# IRELAND

## A PICTURE MEMORY

Published in Ireland by
Gill and Macmillan Ltd
Goldenbridge
Dublin 8
with associated companies in
Auckland, Dallas, Delhi, Hong Kong,
Johannesburg, Lagos, London, Manzini,
Melbourne, Nairobi, New York, Singapore,
Tokyo, Washington
© Photographs, 1991, Colour Library Books Ltd, Godalming, Surrey, England
© Text, 1991, Gill and Macmillan
Printed and bound in Hong Kong
ISBN 0 7171 1873 8

# IRELAND

## A PICTURE MEMORY

**Gill and Macmillan**

For thousands of years, Ireland was the edge of the known world. The island lies on the most westerly tip of the vast Eurasian landmass. To the west, there is nothing except the Atlantic Ocean. To the east there is another small island, Britain, and then beyond that the great North European plain runs away to the Ural Mountains. Beyond the Urals, Siberia folds around the curve of the world until it reaches the Bering Strait, almost touching Alaska. For most of human history, therefore, Ireland was at the very edge of the known world.

The Romans, who went just about everywhere, never bothered with Ireland. After all, everyone knew that Ireland was just an island on the edge of nowhere. Everyone, that is, except the Irish, who were certain that there was something out there beyond the ocean. They proved it, too. It is widely believed that Irishman St Brendan discovered America a thousand years before Columbus sailed.

Like St Brendan, the Irish have always been curious about the outside world. They have not always been willing emigrants, but they have been remarkably successful ones. Today, in the United States alone, forty million people are proud to claim Irish descent, and all around the world there is ample testimony to the intelligence, hard work and determination of Irish people.

Ireland is her people. But the Irish people are, in turn, formed by the magnificent combination of landscape and climate that is the island of Ireland. The country is a mixture of magnificent mountains, rolling and fertile plains and clear, unpolluted rivers and lakes. Although the Irish often complain about the weather, they are in fact blessed with one of the most benign climates in the world. There are no extremes of heat or cold, and when the sun shines, it is a paradise.

Perhaps it is this temperate and gentle climate that gives the country and the people their character. Ireland is relaxed and easy-going, not given to hurry or excess and always ready with a welcome for the stranger. *Céad mile fáilte* is the traditional Gaelic greeting: a hundred thousand welcomes. So it has always been and always will be.

That ready greeting, that hand extended to the visitor, is the modern version of Ireland's eternal curiosity about other people and other places. For it is, as millions of visitors to Ireland over the years can verify, something sincere and genuine. It is neither forced nor manufactured. When an Irish person tells you that you are welcome, it is meant from the heart. Like every country, Ireland has its faults but cynicism in its people is not one of them.

So relax and enjoy the country where time goes more slowly and the people are more friendly and life is gentler than anywhere else you have ever been. See the magnificent and majestic scenery of Kerry and Cork, with Killarney – 'heaven's reflection' – at its centre. Visit rugged Connemara and, just to the north of it, the lakes of Mayo and the Yeats country. Travel the stunningly beautiful coast of Donegal, or the Glens of Antrim, two of Ireland's best kept secrets. Marvel at the rich river valleys of the southeast and the rolling, fertile fields of the Golden Vale rippling across north Munster from east Tipperary to the very borders of Kerry itself. And don't forget the towns and cities: Dublin, one of the truly great world capitals, sophisticated and yet small enough not to have lost its human dimension; Belfast, a fine Victorian city surrounded by the most gorgeous countryside; Cork, the Venice of the south; Galway, a centre of learning and the arts, with its fabled bay; Limerick, standing proudly at the head of the Shannon estuary – the list goes on.

So welcome to Ireland: *céad mile fáilte*. Ireland is no longer at the edge of the world. It is, in a strange way, the centre of the world. Or at least it is the centre of that world in which people strive to lead a good and decent life, in which human values prevail and where no one is ever too busy to throw you a wave or a greeting. Enjoy it, and when your visit ends you will discover, like so many visitors before you, that you are just a little lonely leaving Ireland. Because Ireland is a kind of home for all of us, a home from home for the human heart.

Left: part of the 100-metre frontage of Queen Elizabeth I's 'College of the Holy and Undivided Trinity', today better known simply as Trinity College, Dublin, the capital's most renowned institute of learning. Here can be seen that world-famous masterpiece of illumination, the Book of Kells, a Latin text of the four Gospels, which lies in the Long Room of the college's library. A leaf of this glisteningly beautiful book is turned daily. The college was founded in 1592 by Queen Elizabeth I and can boast Oliver Goldsmith, Edmund Burke and Oscar Wilde among its graduates. Below: the General Post Office on O'Connell Street. To Irishmen, this building is always known by its initials. It was here that the 1916 Easter Rising took place when its leader, Patrick Pearse and a band of some 150 armed men, simply walked in to the GPO and ordered everybody out. Pearse then read the Proclamation of the Irish Republic and awaited the British troops. They came, and within a fortnight the ringleaders of the rebellion had been executed. With their deaths the dream of an independent Ireland was born. A copy of the Proclamation is displayed in the GPO. Facing page: (top) the Four Courts on the River Liffey and (bottom and overleaf) the bridge and street named after Daniel O'Connell.

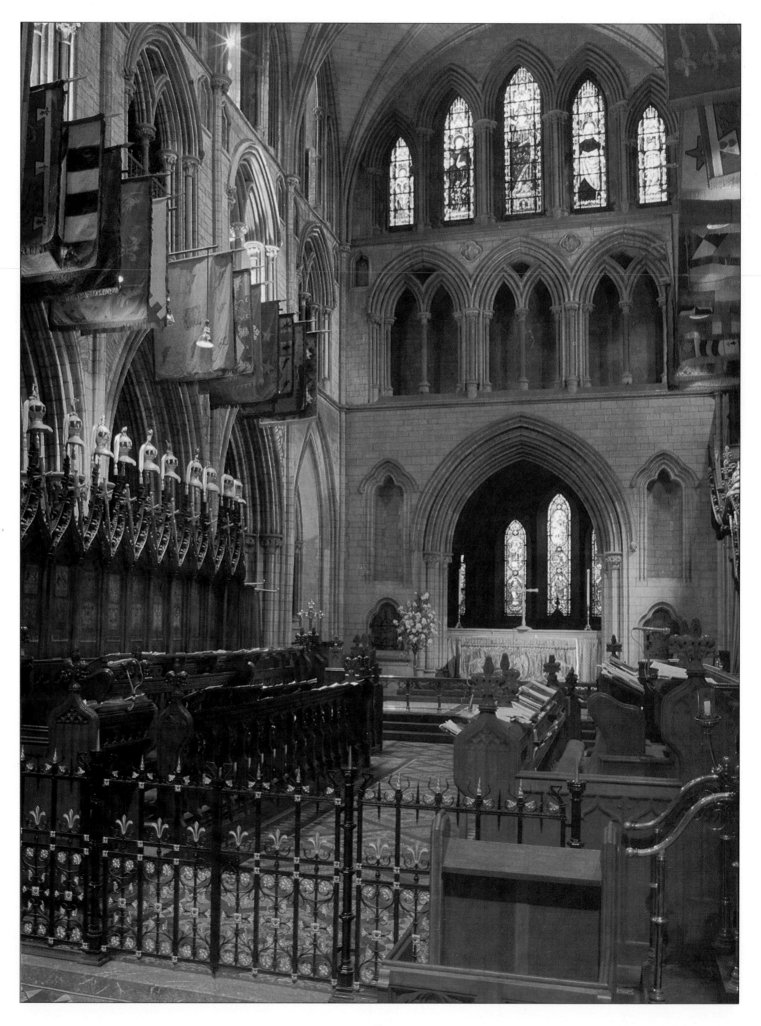

Facing page: St Patrick's Cathedral, Dublin, one of the oldest places of worship in the capital. Dedicated in 1192, the cathedral has been restored many times and since the Reformation has belonged to the Church of Ireland. Jonathan Swift, the renowned satirist who was Dean of the cathedral for over thirty years, is buried here. Above: the ornate and gilt-laden Throne Room, part of the lavish State Apartments designed for English viceroys in Dublin Castle and (below) contrasting simplicity in Ireland's oldest public library, Marsh's Library, where patrons' reading cages – designed to prevent pilferage – are still in place. The library was founded in 1701 by Archbishop Marsh. Right: the appropriately named Long Room, Trinity College, Dublin, lined with marble busts of the college's famous alumni. Here can be found four Shakespeare folios, as well as the Book of Kells.

Above: a splendid door and (below left) an ornate floor, typical of the surroundings that provide elegant backdrops for the exhibits in Dublin's National Museum (below). Above left: *The Wrestlers*, a copy of a marble sculpture by Piamontini in the National Gallery, which boasts works by Rembrandt, El Greco and Degas, as well as a number by Irish artists such as Jack B. Yeats and Walter Osborne. Facing page: the National Library, a comprehensive treasure house of information about Ireland.

13

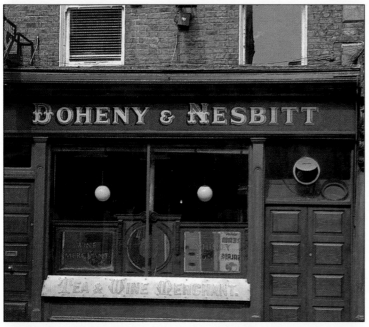

Facing page: Dublin shops and pubs. Unlike English pubs, Irish bars have no signs outside and, to the uninitiated, they look like shops. Once inside, though, it is clear where one is (below).

Right: marigolds in Merrion Square, where Yeats once lived. Below: Dublin's Grand Canal, an eighteenth-century waterway which connects Dublin Bay with the mighty River Shannon. Now closed to commercial traffic, it has become a place for quiet walks, seeming almost rural in nature along some of its length. Equally restful is the city's huge park, Phoenix Park (below right and bottom right) – the largest enclosed park in any European city. It contains, among other features, a herd of fallow deer, a zoo, a polo ground and the residence of the Irish premier.

Below: a horse grazes in the Vale of Clara (left), and (below left) autumn tints the surroundings of the 1000-year-old Round Tower at Glendalough Monastery, both in County Wicklow.

Right and top: glass-making at the Waterford Glass works. The factory can be visited during working hours, when informative guides lead the way through the processes of glass blowing, polishing and cutting. A display of crystal produced at the works can be examined in the entrance hall, where a magnificent collection of intricate chandeliers (above) presides over all.

Above left: the ruins of Muckross Abbey and (above) well-preserved Muckross House, both near Killarney in County Kerry. Left and below: Ashford Castle on the shores of Lough Corrib near Cong, County Mayo. The castle, once owned by the Guinness family, is today a hotel that holds the distinction of having been thought one of the best in the British Isles by Egon Ronay. At its gates lie the ruins of a twelfth-century Augustinian abbey (facing page bottom right), part of which has been reconstructed. Facing page: (top left, top right and bottom left) Blarney Castle, which lies northwest of Cork. One of the most famous ruins in Ireland, Blarney Castle is visited annually by thousands wishing to kiss the Blarney Stone and so, according to the legend, acquire the gift of eloquence. Overleaf: Cork pastureland.

Cork (these pages), the second largest city in the Republic of Ireland, lies on an island in the River Lee and has been been christened the 'Paris of Ireland' for its beauty. Below: Cork's Father Mathew Memorial Church, named for the founder of the Irish temperance movement. Overleaf: St Colman's Cathedral overlooks the harbour in Cobh, County Cork.

Facing page: a rainbow – a common sight in this land of showers – arching over St Mary's Cathedral in Killarney, County Kerry. Below: fishing boats huddle in Dingle Harbour, the most westerly harbour in Europe, County Kerry. Bottom left: Dingle's unassuming Main Street contrasts with the bustle of Castle Street (bottom right) in Tralee, Kerry's industrial centre.

Left: foaming seas off Coumeenoole Strand on the Dingle Peninsula (these pages), County Kerry. The Peninsula has as its spine the rounded peaks of the Slieve Mish range. This chain stretches the strip of land nearly fifty kilometres out to sea and holds, at its tip, the westernmost habitations of Europe. Bottom: the view from Smerwick Harbour towards Kilmalkedar.

These pages: the Dingle Peninsula, County Kerry. The beaches in the west of Ireland are some of the finest in Europe, but they remain undisturbed because, although the country is washed by the Gulf Stream, a dip in the sea remains a bracing experience. Nevertheless, on a sunny day a beach as fine as Coumeenoole Strand (bottom and right) will draw numerous visitors.

In Ireland, ruins and ancient remains may be found around any corner. On the Dingle Peninsula (these pages) the stone that is such a feature of the landscape of Kerry has been used to fashion walls and houses that seem as natural as their surroundings. Bottom left: the Gallarus Oratory, a remarkable survival from early Christian times, which lies near Ballyferriter.

Left and below: the undeniably romantic ramparts of the Cliffs of Moher, which defy the Atlantic north of Liscannor in County Clare. In places they rise sheer for over 200 metres. Bottom: a blacksmith uses the age-old tools of his trade at his forge in Bunratty, County Clare. In Ireland, where there's a horse to be found in most villages, the smith is an important man.

Facing page: a fisherman waits hopefully beside the torrent of the Owenriff River in County Galway. Above: white water spills from Ballynahinch Lough and (right) hay dries in Roundstone, both in Joyce Country, Connemara, one of the loneliest and loveliest regions of Ireland. Below: a solitary cottage near Leenane, County Galway, which could belong to the last, rather than the present, century. Overleaf: Lough Corrib, County Galway.

Above: a traditional Irish sailing boat, known as a hooker, in Carna, County Galway. Such vessels often dock in Roundstone harbour (above left and left), Bertraghboy Bay (below left) and other Galway ports of call. Below: a cockerel struts in front of Maumeen Lough and the Twelve Bens, or Pins, of Connemara beyond. These peaks, which change colour with the light and the season, are part of the Benna Beola range. Facing page: a lone rowing boat lies in shadow as sunshine falls on the green shores of Westport Bay near Murrisk in County Mayo.

Below and bottom left: tranquil water reflects a rich blend of greens and blues – the colours of the Irish countryside – at Killary Harbour, which forms part of the county boundary between Mayo and Galway. Below left: donkeys graze and gaze beside Kingstown Bay (left), which lies west of Clifden in Connemara, a region better known for the world-famous Connemara pony than for these humble beasts of burden.

Below: a white statue of St Patrick, the patron saint of Ireland, overlooks Clew Bay at the foot of Croagh Patrick, a 762-metre-high mountain in County Mayo. A conical peak, the mountain is considered to be holy, since legend has it that Saint Patrick spent forty days here in prayer and fasting for the people of Ireland. Bottom right: Ashleagh Falls, near Leenane, and (remaining pictures) timeless rural scenes, all in County Mayo.

Facing page centre right: a Donegal donkey. Remaining pictures:
Donegal men, working and resting. Though farming may look
idyllic, it is hard work – especially at haymaking and harvest.

Left: Adare Manor, a Neo-Gothic mansion built by the third Earl of Dunraven, who also built a row of cottages in Adare, County Limerick, for his tenants. Unlike many Englishmen, the earl was a popular landlord; his son went on to instigate the 1903 act that enabled tenants to buy the land they farmed. Below: the River Blackwater, County Meath, and (bottom) Birr Castle, County Offaly. Overleaf: the Cooley Peninsula, County Louth.

Above: a waterfall in the Glencar Lakes area of County Leitrim and (below) Lough Key Forest Park, one of many state-owned recreation areas in County Sligo. Above left: the limestone rock formation known as the Wishing Arch, visible from the Antrim coast road, a route which affords the walker spectacular views of brown moorlands, white limestone, black basalt, red sandstone and blue sea. The road, a notable engineering achievement, was built in 1834 to provide work for famine victims and opened up an area whose inhabitants had previously found it easier to travel by sea to Scotland than overland to the rest of Ireland. Left: golfers on the green in County Monaghan. Golf is a national passion and is played by everyone in Ireland sufficiently interested to buy a set of clubs; the country is dotted with golf courses. Facing page: the rope bridge at Carrick-a-rede, near Ballintoy, County Antrim. Visitors view this slim bridge, which is taken down during the winter months, when the winds become severe, with some trepidation. Locals, however, happily cross it, maintaining their balance despite the considerable sway their speed produces. Below left: fishing boats cluster in Kilkeel Harbour after braving the fierce Irish Sea. Kilkeel, in County Down, lies at the foot of the beautiful Mountains of Mourne. Overleaf: sea pinks brighten an overcast day at White Rocks on the Antrim coast.

# "55'n Smiling" DISCOUNTS

# IRELAND & BRITAIN

 **C·I·E TOURS International**

**Aer Lingus**

**1991**

# SAVE...on Great New Air/Land Prices

New for 1991—Special new low air fares mean great savings for you.

CIE Tours and Aer Lingus have come together to bring you combined Air/Land Inclusive Prices at the best value available. And you have the extra security of knowing that you fly with Ireland's national flag carrier and tour with Ireland's national transportation company. Your agent knows the reputation for quality which CIE Tours have earned over 57 years of providing the very best in touring to discriminating American tourists to Ireland and Britain.

**Fares from your Home City**
Special APEX fares are available from many American cities to Dublin and Shannon in conjunction with Aer Lingus and a selection of American carriers. Ask your Travel Agent for the best fare base from your city.
You'll be surprised at the great value available.

## Aer Lingus

## - A Little Bit of Ireland

Aer Lingus operates more flights to Ireland than any other airline. They also operate a full schedule of frequent services to Britain and mainland Europe. There's one lovely line that says it all: "Look up, it's Aer Lingus, there's a little bit of Ireland passing by". It's so true. The moment you step on board your Aer Lingus flight at Boston, New York or Chicago, it's like stepping into Ireland itself. You sit down, take the weight off your feet, relax and enjoy the friendly attention of your Irish cabin attendants. Dinner and continental breakfast is served on board.

## CONTENTS

## OUR GUARANTEE:
## THE BEST AIR FARE!!
Fares quoted for Air/Land Inclusive Programs are the very best available at time of printing—in fact we have reduced them in many cases to save you as much as $50 per couple—but if the airlines offer lower fares before you book—you'll get the best available at that time.
**—That's Our Guarantee!**

# REAL $$ VALUE AND QUALITY . . .

## Your C.I.E. Tours Guarantee

The number of American clients selecting CIE Tours for their Irish & British vacations increased by more than 35% in 1990. Some people would say "If it ain't broke, don't fix it". But we've taken the other approach - "Let's improve it". And that's exactly what we've done. We've planned a bigger and better selection of tour programs for 1991. Combination Britain/Ireland Car Package (Pages 6 & 7) & a new tour of all of Ireland (Page 16). More discounts for those "55 'n Smiling", new extras added to tours & new inclusive Air/Land Programs from Chicago. We think you'll find exactly what you want right here - Value & Quality backed by 57 years of reliability.

### QUALITY

Compare the range and the quality of our hotels, the visits and extras on our tours with offers in other brochures to Ireland and you'll see immediately that CIE Tours is the quality tour operator. We set the standards that others follow and our policy is to ensure you have a real value, quality vacation.

### WHAT WE MEAN BY REAL VALUE

For example, on your CIE Tours motorcoach vacation, a full Irish breakfast means exactly that—a choice of cereals, juice, Irish bacon and eggs etc., not just coffee and croissants, continental style. And when it comes to evening dinner at your hotel, you'll have a wide choice from a Table d'hote dinner menu.

Another example is that many of our Irish coach tours include a Mediaeval Banquet in an Irish Castle and an Irish Ceili (that's an Irish Hooley!) with dinner and entertainment as well as lots of other extras—Abbey Theater, Blarney Castle, Jaunting Car Tour of Killarney and other features. And we are not finished yet. Our very popular Irish Tradition tours include a very special dinner in Dublin's most elegant seafood restaurant, followed by a visit to the world renowned Abbey Theater.

### DISCOUNTS—IF YOU'RE "55 'N SMILING"

If you are 55 or older we have a present for you: $100 and $75 discounts off selected departures on a number of escorted tours. See Pages 10/11, 14/15 & 16.

### AND THAT'S NOT ALL . . .

Our self-drive vacations include unique extras:
—You'll receive a full 60 minute audio tape on Ireland and Britain, filled with useful hints and information to help you plan your vacation.
—Your free, super full color souvenier Atlas Touring Guide of Ireland (when you pick up your car on arrival in Ireland).

**No tour operator gives you both of these—FREE!!!**

### SECURITY ASSURED

As a U.S. registered company for over 25 years, and as an associate of Ireland's National Transport Company, you can be sure of our reliability and security.

### EXPERIENCE

CIE TOURS have been arranging vacations in Europe for over 57 years. Over ONE MILLION passengers—many of them return guests—have travelled with us, and each year over 30,000 U.S. and Canadian visitors enjoy our range of vacations.

### LUXURY COACHES

When you tour with CIE Tours you'll travel in the height of luxury—Luxury Touring Coaches—Panoramic Windows—Reclining Seats—Individual Air Control.

### YOUR FRIEND BEHIND THE WHEEL

You will be in the hands of capable and skilled professionals who know every inch of Ireland and Britain. "Patience", "Friendliness"& "Informative" are the characteristics that best describe this very special group of people, they are full of humour and wit and use it generously while informing you of every aspect of life in these lands.

# SELF DRIVE VACATIONS IN IRELAND

## Stay at Friendly Farmhouses and Town & Country Homes...

CIE Tours makes it all so easy. Our Go-As-You-Please Vacations include a current model car and vouchers to cover accommodation at a Farmhouse or Town & Country Home each night, together with full Irish breakfast each morning.

A 128 Page Atlas Guide to help you make the most of your time and an audio cassette tape sent to you "in advance of your trip—full of hints and help".

Located throughout the north & south of Ireland over 1100 homes offer a refreshing and unique experience to the visitor. The accommodation, although simple, is of a very high standard and subject to regular Tourist Board inspections.

*Exploring Aviation History at Shannon.*

### LIKE TO TRY OUR HOTELS?
While on your Farmhouse Vacation would you like to spend one or more nights at one of our Go-As-You-Please Hotels, or at a Castle? Simply present your voucher to the hotel or castle concerned and pay the *discounted* upgrade supplement. You'll receive with your farmhouse documentation full details of all hotels and castles—phone #'s & supplements.

### YOUR PRICE INCLUDES:
★ **Round Trip Flight** from U.S. to Shannon by Aer Lingus with dinner & continental breakfast on board.
★ **Self Drive Car** standard shift Ford Fiesta (or similar Group "A" current model.)
★ **Pick-up & drop off without charge** in Shannon, Dublin or Cork.
★ **Unlimited mileage & Government Tax (VAT)** on car rental.
★ **Accommodation** for duration of your stay at friendly Farmhouses, Town & Country Homes.
★ **Full Irish Breakfast daily** (except day of arrival).
★ **FIRST NIGHT PRE-BOOKED** ON REQUEST. CIE TOURS WILL RESERVE FREE OF CHARGE YOUR FIRST NIGHT'S ACCOMMODATION IN SHANNONSIDE AT TIME OF BOOKING VACATION ONLY.
★ **Free souvenier Irish Touring Guide and Atlas** (one per couple).
★ **Free CIE Tours exclusive "Touring through the Treasure Isles" audio tape** - a lively 60 minute program of travel hints (one per couple).
★ **Complimentary gift** at Gap of Dunloe Industries, Killarney.
★ **All local taxes** and guided tour of Royal Tara China Factory.
★ **Three persons** travelling together, and occupying triple room throughout, will receive a standard-shift Ford Orion (or similar group "C" rental car) at **no extra charge.**
★ **Four persons** travelling together, & booking 2 twin bedded rooms, will receive a standard-shift Ford Sierra (or similar group "D" rental car) at **no extra charge.**
★ **Automatic cars** available on request.

### SAVE...SAVE...SAVE...

**• SAVE UP TO $120 ON YOUR C.D.W. CHARGES WITH CIE TOURS**

Many of the major credit card companies offer Collision Damage Waiver protection on your car hire. If you have this entitlement, you are welcome to use it with your CIE Tours car program and you can save from $90 to $120 C.D.W. charge which some operators will be charging. Check your credit card company and also your own insurance company conditions on C.D.W. before you travel. If you have this entitlement, you may avail of it by simply presenting your card at Dublin or Shannon Airport Car Hire Desk—and save with us.

**• FREE SOUVENIR IRISH TOURING GUIDE AND ATLAS**

Published specially for CIE Tours, and designed to enhance your Irish vacation, the latest book on Ireland by Hugh Oram, a distinguished travel writer, is yours FREE on your tour (on arrival in Ireland when you pick up your car). Retail value in shops $20 approx.

**FARMHOUSES/TOWN & COUNTRY HOMES—PRICE PER PERSON**  IT 1 El 19122

TOUR PKBB

| Number of persons | JAN 1—JUNE 14 NOV 1—DEC 13 | | | | | JUNE 15—SEPT 15 | | | | | SEPT. 16—OCT. 31 | | | | |
|---|---|---|---|---|---|---|---|---|---|---|---|---|---|---|---|
| | 4 Days Land (3N) | 1 Wk. Land Price (6N) | 1 Wk. Incl.Air JFK/Bos (6N) | 1 Wk. Incl.Air Chic. (6N) | Extra Day (1N) | 4 Days Land (3N) | 1 Wk. Land Price (6N) | 1 Wk. Incl.Air JFK/Bos (6N) | 1 Wk. Incl.Air Chic. (6N) | Extra Day (1N) | 4 Days Land (3N) | 1 Wk. Land Price (6N) | 1 Wk. Incl.Air JFK/Bos. (6N) | 1 Wk. Incl.Air Chic. (6N) | Extra Day (1N) |
| 4 | $151 | $267 | $834 | $897 | $43 | $163 | $289 | $964 | $964 | $45 | $159 | $279 | $846 | $909 | $45 |
| 3 | 165 | 289 | 856 | 919 | 46 | 171 | 299 | 974 | 974 | 49 | 162 | 289 | 856 | 919 | 47 |
| 2 | 168 | 292 | 859 | 922 | 46 | 190 | 324 | 999 | 999 | 49 | 177 | 310 | 877 | 940 | 47 |
| 1 | 237 | 395 | 962 | 1025 | 64 | 279 | 459 | 1134 | 1134 | 73 | 249 | 415 | 982 | 1045 | 67 |

**SINGLE ROOM SUPPLEMENT:** $10 per person per night (this is not included in "One Person" price above.) **CHILDREN'S RATES:** When sharing room with adults deduct $5 per night.
**INCLUSIVE AIR PRICES:** Are based on Aer Lingus non-refundable fares to Shannon (see conditions). **WEEKEND SURCHARGES:** June 15—Aug. 31 (only) JFK/BOS. $14 per journey, Chicago $23 per journey. **DUBLIN ADD-ONS:** Add $15 each way to or from Dublin. **SEPT. 1—15:** Deduct $108 JFK/BOS., deduct $45 Chicago from above fares. Standard APEX fares available on request. U.S. Airport Tax $16 not included.

# SELF DRIVE VACATIONS IN IRELAND

## Stay at First Class Hotels...

### SAVE...SAVE...SAVE...

**• NO HIDDEN TAX CHARGES**
For example, Government Tax (VAT) on car rental in Europe is usually added to the cost of your vacation when you collect your car. We don't do that. Instead we make it easy by INCLUDING VAT in the cost of all our tours.

**• 1ST NIGHT PRE-BOOKED FREE**
CIE Tours will reserve free of charge your first night's accommodation at Shannon on request at time of booking your vacation.

**FREE "TOURING THROUGH THE TREASURE ISLES"—Audio Tape**
A lively 60-minute audio tape of hints and advice specially produced by CIE Tours to help you plan your trip. You'll receive your copy BEFORE YOU TRAVEL and then you can sit back at leisure, in the company of the experts, as they answer your questions on driving, dining, shopping, where to go and what to do.

**SELF-DRIVE ONLY - RATES**
Please see Page 22.

If you prefer to stay at some of Ireland's finest and friendliest hotels during your visit, you can do so with CIE Tours— Because we have carefully selected over 150 quality hotels. No part of the Emerald Isle is missed—North, South, East or West. You won't find a more comprehensive list of hotels anywhere. Our documentation/ information kit is simplicity itself—Like to stay in a castle? Or in a farmhouse? You can do so with ease with the CIE Tours Go-As-You-Please Hotel Program. We'll give you a current model self-drive car together with voucher for room (with bath) and full breakfast daily—a 128 page Atlas Guide— your audio cassette tape in advance—and off you go.

---

**Experience the Luxury of an Irish Castle or Manor House**

Ashford, Dromoland or Waterford Castles— Adare Manor, Mount Juliet. Present your Go-As-You-Please voucher and pay the supplement directly. **Details in your Travel Documents.**

---

**Spend a night at a Farmhouse—**
While on your hotel vacation would you like to spend a night at a farmhouse? Simply present your hotel voucher to the "Bean A'Ti"-"Woman of the House" you'll get room, full home-cooked breakfast AND dinner—at no extra cost. You'll get with your documents full farmhouse details, addresses, phone numbers, etc.

**YOUR PRICE INCLUDES:**
★ **Round Trip Flight** from U.S. to Shannon by Aer Lingus with dinner and continental breakfast on board.
★ **Self Drive Car** standard shift Ford Fiesta (or similar group "A" current model).
★ **Pick-up and drop off without charge** in Shannon, Dublin or Cork.
★ **Unlimited mileage & Government Tax (VAT) on car rental.**
★ **Accommodation** for duration of your stay at hotels in rooms with private bath or shower.
★ **Full Irish Breakfast daily** (except day of arrival).
★ **FIRST NIGHT PRE-BOOKED** ON REQUEST. CIE TOURS WILL RESERVE FREE OF CHARGE YOUR FIRST NIGHT'S ACCOMMODATION IN SHANNONSIDE OR DUBLIN AREAS AT TIME OF BOOKING VACATION ONLY.
★ **Free souvenir Irish Touring Guide and Atlas** (one per couple).
★ **Free CIE Tours exclusive "Touring through the Treasure Isles" audio tape** - a lively 60 minute program of travel hints (one per couple).
★ **All local taxes** and a guided tour of Royal Tara China Factory.
★ **Complimentary gift** at Gap of Dunloe Industries, Killarney.
★ **Three persons** travelling together, and occupying triple room throughout, will receive a standard-shift Ford Orion (or similar group "C" rental car) at **no extra charge.**
★ **Four persons** travelling together, and booking two twin bedded rooms, will receive a standard-shift Ford Sierra (or similar group "D" rental car) at **no extra charge.**
★ **Automatic cars** available on request.

---

| HOTELS—PRICE PER PERSON | IT 1 EI 19121 | | | | | | | | | | | | | | TOUR PKAA |
|---|---|---|---|---|---|---|---|---|---|---|---|---|---|---|---|
| Number of persons | JAN 1—JUNE 14 NOV 1—DEC 13 | | | | | JUNE 15—SEPT 15 | | | | | SEPT. 16—OCT. 31 | | | | |
| | 4 Days Land (3N) | 1 Wk. Land Price (6N) | 1 Wk. Incl.Air JFK/Bos. (6N) | 1 Wk. Incl.Air Chic. (6N) | Extra Day (1N) | 4 Days Land (3N) | 1 Wk. Land Price (6N) | 1 Wk. Incl.Air JFK/Bos (6N) | 1 Wk. Incl.Air Chic. (6N) | Extra Day (1N) | 4 Days Land (3N) | 1 Wk. Land Price (6N) | 1 Wk. Incl.Air JFK/Bos. (6N) | 1 Wk. Incl.Air Chic. (6N) | Extra Day (1N) |
| 4 | $224 | $399 | $966 | $1029 | $64 | $266 | $465 | $1140 | $1140 | $75 | $239 | $435 | $1002 | $1065 | $69 |
| 3 | 239 | 425 | 992 | 1055 | 67 | 277 | 479 | 1154 | 1154 | 77 | 245 | 435 | 1002 | 1065 | 69 |
| 2 | 242 | 429 | 996 | 1059 | 68 | 289 | 499 | 1174 | 1174 | 79 | 259 | 449 | 1016 | 1079 | 69 |
| 1 | 305 | 529 | 1096 | 1159 | 84 | 375 | 615 | 1290 | 1290 | 99 | 325 | 549 | 1116 | 1179 | 87 |

**SINGLE ROOM SUPPLEMENT:** $20 per person per night (this is not included in "One Person" price above.) **CHILDREN'S RATES:** When sharing room with adults deduct $16 per night.
**INCLUSIVE AIR PRICES:** Are based on Aer Lingus non-refundable fares to Shannon (see conditions). **WEEKEND SURCHARGES:** June 15—Aug. 31 (only) JFK/BOS. $14 per journey.
Chicago $23 per journey. **DUBLIN ADD-ONS:** Add $15 each way to or from Dublin. **SEPT. 1—15:** Deduct $108 JFK/BOS., deduct $45 Chicago from above fares. Standard APEX fares available on request. U.S. Airport Tax $16 not included.

# BRITAIN & IRELAND COMBINED VACATIONS
## GO-AS-YOU-PLEASE SELF DRIVE
## STAY IN FARMHOUSES/GUESTHOUSES OR HOTELS

We call it our "Go As You Please" program because that is just what it means—it gives you the key to carefree and independent driving throughout Britain and Ireland. Although in Britain and Ireland we drive on the left side, the roads are relatively traffic-free and you'll adjust quickly. The roads are well maintained and clearly signposted and most distances are short. Travel from city to city, country to country, drive on the motorways and country roads, meander in the towns and villages, or blend a bit of everything along the route. You can explore the great historic sights of Britain and Ireland or just get off the beaten track and visit the thatched cottages, castles, farmhouses and manor homes.

*Rock of Cashel · Co. Tipperary.*

## HOTELS

Value and variety are the keynotes of this flexible Go As You Please Vacation of Britain and Ireland combined. We have made special arrangements for you at over 300 great hotels from the Consort Hotel Group. This consortium of independent hotels, many managed by the owners, are strategically located to allow you to tour the most scenic and interesting places throughout Britain - from modern city center to historic coaching inns. In Ireland, 150 hotels selected to make it easy and enjoyable for you to experience the beauty and serenity of Ireland.

*Beer and Skittles, English Style*

## FARMHOUSE/GUESTHOUSE

If you really want to experience the history, the folklore and the legends of Britain and Ireland, then there's no better way than to stay in the homes of the people.

CIE Tours International offers you a great choice of accommodations —in Britain, four star category farms and country homes throughout England, Scotland and Wales—all different but all providing good food, warm hospitality and a unique insight into the British way of life. In Ireland, You'll stay at friendly farmhouses and town and country homes—located throughout Ireland, over 750 homes offer a refreshing and unique experience to visitors.

And CIE Tours "Great Meet the People" go as you please vacation of Britain and Ireland makes it all possible. We'll provide you with a current model car in each country, vouchers to cover your overnight's accommodations each night with full breakfast each morning, your personal atlas guide of Ireland, map of Britain, and accommodation lists. In addition, you'll have CIE's exclusive Treasure Isles Touring audio-tape—60 lively minutes of travel hints. You'll receive your copy as soon as you book your vacation and then you can sit back at leisure, in the company of experts, as they answer your questions about touring in Britain and Ireland.

## YOUR PRICE INCLUDES:

★ **Round trip flight** from U.S. (including flight UK/Ireland).
★ **Self Drive Car** standard shift Ford Fiesta (or similar Group "A" model) in Britain and Ireland.
★ **Unlimited mileage.**
★ **Accommodation for 6 nights** (minimum 3 nights Britain and 3 nights Ireland) at four star farmhouses in Britain and town & country homes in Ireland or in your choice of hotels.
★ **First night** pre-booked in Manchester OR London OR in Shannonside. CIE will reserve free of charge your first night's accommodation at Manchester OR London OR Shannonside areas at time of booking vacation only.
★ **Full breakfast daily** (Continental breakfast only in London).
★ **CIE Tours' exclusive** "Touring through the Treasure Isles" audio tape—a lively 60-minute program of travel hints (one per couple).
★ **Your personal Atlas Guide** in Ireland and free map in Britain (one per couple).
★ **Pick up and drop off** car without charge at either Shannon or Dublin (Irl)or Lon/Man/Gla (UK) airports.
★ **Automobile Club (RAC)**—24 hour emergency service in Britain—Tipperary Car Hire Emergency Service throughout Ireland.
★ **Hotel service charges** and Government Tax (V.A.T.) on car and accommodation.

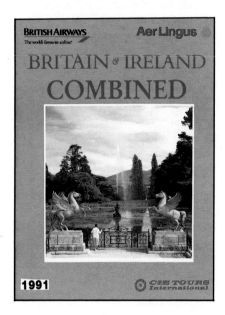

PRICE PER PERSON (minimum 3 nights Britain & 3 nights Ireland)

| | Tour PKFY No. of Per. traveling | APRIL & NOVEMBER | | | | MAY & OCT. | | | | JUNE—SEPT. | | | |
|---|---|---|---|---|---|---|---|---|---|---|---|---|---|
| FARMHOUSE VACATION | | Lnd.Only (6N) | Air/Lnd Incl. | Ex.Nt. Irl. | Ex.Nt. Brit. | Lnd.Only (6N) | Air/Lnd. Incl. | Ex.Nt. Irl. | Ex.Nt. Brit. | Lnd.Only (6N) | Air/Lnd. Incl. | Ex.Nt. Irl. | Ex.Nt. Brit. |
| | 4 | $373 | $1193 | $43 | $66 | $374 | $1194 | $43 | $68 | $386 | $1272 | $45 | $68 |
| | 3 | 387 | 1207 | 46 | 67 | 394 | 1214 | 46 | 68 | 400 | 1286 | 49 | 68 |
| | 2 | 393 | 1213 | 46 | 68 | 400 | 1220 | 46 | 69 | 422 | 1308 | 49 | 69 |
| HOTEL VACATION | Tour PKHX | Lnd.Only (6N) | Air/Ind. Incl. | Ex.Day Irl. | Ex.Day Brit. | Lnd.Only (6N) | Air/Lnd. Incl. | Ex.Day Irl. | Ex.Day Brit. | Lnd.Only | Air/Lnd. Incl. | Ex.Day Irl. | Ex.Day Brit. |
| | 4 | 455 | 1275 | 64 | 70 | 492 | 1312 | 69 | 78 | 519 | 1405 | 75 | 78 |
| | 3 | 472 | 1292 | 67 | 70 | 504 | 1324 | 69 | 78 | 536 | 1422 | 77 | 78 |
| | 2 | 478 | 1298 | 68 | 71 | 521 | 1341 | 69 | 79 | 551 | 1437 | 79 | 79 |

**TOUR PKFY:** Single room supplement in Ireland $10 nightly, pay direct in Britain. **CHILDREN REDUCTION:** $10 nightly when sharing room with adults. **TOUR PKHX:** Single room supplement in Ireland $20 nightly, in Britain pay direct (¶10 sterling nightly.) **INCLUSIVE AIR:** Prices are based on standard APEX Tariffs from JFK/BOSTON to London or from JFK to Glasgow. **WEEKEND TRAVEL:** Weekend air supplement of $27 each way. From your home city ask for details of special fares. Non-refundable air fares are available—ask for details. U.S. Airport Tax $16 not included.

# IRISH HERITAGE

**A quality tour with superb hotels and entertainment - escorted by your CIE Tour Director and Driver.**
**8 or 9 Days Vacation ★ ★ ★ ★ ★**
**FROM—$769**

Long established as the most popular tour for visitors from North America, this vacation is designed to give you a glimpse of Ireland through the ages - you'll feast at a 15th century banquet in an Irish Castle, ride in a jaunting car around the lakes of Killarney, visit landmarks like Blarney Castle, Muckross House Folk Museum, and above all, your heart will be warmed by the welcoming hospitality of the Irish people. You'll meet the Irish at a working farm and enjoy tea and scones. You'll stay in quality first class hotels, escorted throughout by friendly professionals - your CIE Tour Director and Driver.

**YOUR ITINERARY:**

**DAY 1—SATURDAY: Depart U.S. for Shannon, Ireland**
Welcome aboard your Aer Lingus flight to Shannon. Dinner and continental breakfast on board.

**DAY 2—SUNDAY: Arrival Shannonside · Mediaeval Splendour**
The tour starts at Shannon Airport. You overnight in the Clare Inn Hotel eight miles away in the green heart of Ireland. This evening, after a restful afternoon, a sumptuous Mediaeval Banquet in a 15th century Irish Castle.

**DAY 3—MONDAY: Majestic Cliffs of Moher & The Lakes of Killarney**
Your day begins with a trip to the mighty Cliffs of Moher, 700 feet over the pounding Atlantic waves, and then southwards through Co. Clare, where we have time to visit Bunratty Cottage Shop. You'll pass through historic Limerick City and the fairytale village of Adare before continuing to Killarney's Lakes and Fells.

**DAY 4—TUESDAY: The Ring of Kerry Tour**
One of the highlights of any European visit lies ahead today - a tour around the unforgettable Ring of Kerry. This 100 mile circular drive is one of the most beautiful trips in the world. You'll visit Muckross House and finish your journey on a horse-drawn jaunting car.

**DAY 5—WEDNESDAY: Blarney Castle & Waterford's Crystal City**
Travel eastwards today to Blarney, where you will acquire the "Gift of Eloquence" by kissing the famous Stone. You'll have time to visit the Blarney Woollen Mills and shop for traditional Irish Handcrafts, knitwear and crystal, before continuing to Cork, and through the ancient town of Youghal to Waterford, famous for its crystal.

**DAY 6—THURSDAY: Historic Kilkenny Castle—Dublin**
From Waterford, home of the famous hand-cut crystal - we may have an opportunity to see it being made - we move north to Kilkenny with its mediaeval streets and buildings. We visit historic Kilkenny Castle, built in the early 13th century and standing on a magnificent site in the southern end of town. Your tour continues to Dublin where this evening, at optional extra cost, you may wish to attend a dinner and lively Irish Cabaret Show at your hotel.

**DAY 7—FRIDAY: Dublin's Fair City**
This morning's sightseeing tour of Dublin, will show you this elegant, artistic city - from the Georgian Squares and buildings to the imposing grandeur of St. Patrick's Cathedral. The afternoon will be left free to browse and shop. Then, to finish the day in style, you'll attend a performance at Dublin's famous Abbey Theater.

**DAY 8—SATURDAY: Tour CDBT (Only) Depart For Home**
Unfortunately, for those on tour CDBT the magic must end today. Your tour will terminate after breakfast at the Burlington Hotel and if you are booked on today's transatlantic flights by CIE Tours, you will be provided with transportation to Dublin Airport.

*A Glimpse of Georgian Dublin.*

*A sightseeing tour of Kilkenny Castle (Day 6)*

**DAY 8—SATURDAY: Tour CDCT (Only) Galway Bay & Connemara**

If you are one of the lucky ones and have another day in Ireland, you'll leave Dublin this morning and travel first across the rolling pastures of Ireland's heartland. Then along the shores of Galway Bay to reach Galway City, capital of the west, shortly after mid-day. Your hotel is in downtown Galway and within walking distance of the memorial to President John F. Kennedy. In the afternoon you'll travel further west into Connemara, a scenic, rugged area, where the Gaelic tongue is still the everyday language.

**DAY 9—SUNDAY: Galway—Shannon—Home**

Bid a farewell this morning to Galway, heart of Connacht, as your coach takes you south to Shannon Airport. The tour terminates in Shannon in time for the principal transatlantic flights. Time for last minute duty free shopping at the extensively stocked Shannon Airport.

**HOTELS:**

You will stay at the following hotels (or hotels of a similar standard):
**Shannonside:** Clare Inn (1 night)
**Killarney:** Great Southern Hotel (2 nights)
**Waterford:** Granville Hotel (1 night)
**Dublin:** Burlington Hotel (2 nights)
**Galway:** Great Southern Hotel (1 night -Tour CDCT only).

**NOTE:**

Departure **Sept. 21** will stay at the Corrib Great Southern Hotel, Galway.

**YOUR PRICE INCLUDES:**

★ **Round trip flight** from U.S. to Shannon by Aer Lingus flight, with dinner & continental breakfast on board.

★ **Sightseeing by luxury coach** throughout your tour.

★ **Professional Irish Tour Director** to escort and entertain you.

★ **Superior first class hotel** accommodation in rooms with private bath or shower.

★ **Full Irish breakfast daily** (except on day of arrival.)

★ **Table d'hote dinner** each evening (except Day 6 & 7)

★ **Mediaeval Banquet** in an Irish Castle.

★ **Reserved seats** at the Abbey Theater.

★ **Tea & scones** at an Irish Farmhouse.

★ **Jaunting car** tour in Killarney.

★ **Visits & admissions** to Muckross House Folk Museum, Blarney Castle, Blarney Woollen Mills, Kilkenny Castle, Waterford Glass Factory (when open), St. Patrick's Cathedral, Galway Cathedral & Celtic Crystal Showrooms, Connemara.

★ **Tips** for baggage handling and to local personnel

★ **All local taxes.**

★ **Deluxe flight bag,** ticket wallet & luggage tags.

*Relaxing with New Friends.*

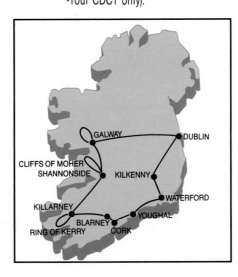

**IRISH HERITAGE TOUR CDBT (8 Day)    IT 1 EI 19107**
**DEPARTURE DATES EX. U.S.A. SATURDAYS: APRIL 06 THRU OCT. 26**

| PRICE PER PERSON SHARING ($US) | LAND COST | INCL. AIR JFK/BOS. | INCL. AIR CHICAGO |
|---|---|---|---|
| April 06—April 27 | $769 | $1351 | $1414 |
| May 04—May 18 | 799 | 1381 | 1444 |
| May 25—June 08 | 895 | 1477 | 1540 |
| June 15—Aug. 31 | 895 | 1613 | 1631 |
| Sept. 07—Sept. 21 | 895 | 1477 | 1540 |
| Sept. 28—Oct. 26 | 799 | 1381 | 1444 |

**TOUR CDCT** (9 Day Vacation) IT 1 EI 19104, add $120 to above land price (but $105 to inclusive air prices). **Single room supplements:** Tour CDBT $190, Tour CDCT $220. **Inclusive Air/Land** prices are based on Aer Lingus non-refundable APEX Fares (see conditions). **Standard APEX** fares available on request. **Note:** Land only departures commence Day 2 Shannon Airport, Ireland. U.S. Departure Tax $16 not included.

# IRISH TRADITION

**A first class tour with four relaxing 2 or 3 night stops - many features and extras.**
**13 Days Vacation ★ ★ ★ ★**
**FROM—$1339      "55 'N SMILING" FROM—$1239**

This comfortably paced leisurely tour of the Emerald Isle features four relaxing 2 or 3 night stops. Stay in first class hotels - a mixture of old world and modern, escorted throughout by an Irish Driver/Guide in your luxury coach. We have included many features and extras on this tour: you'll enjoy a traditional Irish Ceili with dinner, feast at a 16th century castle banquet; visit Dublin's famous Abbey Theater; meet the locals over tea and scones at an Irish Farmhouse; experience a ride around the Killarney lakes in an Irish Jaunting Car; and much more.

**YOUR ITINERARY:**
**DAY 1—SATURDAY: Depart U.S. For Shannon, Ireland**
Welcome aboard your Aer Lingus flight to Shannon. Dinner and continental breakfast on board.

**DAY 2—SUNDAY: Arrival Shannonside—Irish Ceili**
The tour starts at Shannon Airport. You overnight in the Clare Inn Hotel eight miles away in the green heart of Ireland. This evening, you'll be entertained by the local folk to a traditional Irish Ceili of country dancing, singing and music, with dinner and wine included.

**DAY 3—MONDAY: Majestic Cliffs of Moher**
Your day begins with a trip to the mighty Cliffs of Moher, 700 feet over the pounding Atlantic waves, and then southwards through Co. Clare, where you have time to visit Bunratty Cottage Shop. You'll pass through historic Limerick City and the fairytale village of Adare before continuing to Killarney.

**DAY 4—TUESDAY: The Ring of Kerry Tour**
The "Ring of Kerry" drive takes you around the beautiful Iveragh Peninsula. A round trip of over 100 miles, with changing views of seascapes and mountain ranges at almost every turn. You'll visit Muckross House and finish your journey on a horse drawn jaunting car.

**DAY 5—WEDNESDAY: Blarney Castle & Waterford's Crystal City**
Eastwards to Cork, on the River Lee. At Blarney Castle, you will acquire the "Gift of Eloquence" bestowed upon you when you kiss the magic Blarney Stone. To Waterford, of Crystal fame,and then to Kilkenny with its mediaeval streets and buildings.

**DAY 6—THURSDAY: Kilkenny Castle & The Garden of Ireland**
This morning we visit historic Kilkenny Castle and then travel through Wicklow "the Garden of Ireland" in the heart of the Wicklow Mountains, where we visit the remains of 6th century Glendalough, with its round tower and chapels. Onwards to Dublin's Fair City. Tonight in Howth, you'll enjoy dinner and a music session at the renowned Abbey Tavern.

**DAY 7—FRIDAY: Dublin's Fair City**
This morning is free to explore Dublin's Fair City: step out into elegant Georgian Squares, fashionable shops and busy arcades. This afternoon's city sightseeing tour includes a visit to St. Patrick's Cathedral. Then this evening, there's an optional visit (at extra cost) to Doyle's Irish Cabaret.

**DAY 8—SATURDAY: Beautiful Dublin Bay**
Today, a guided tour on the Dublin Area Rapid Transit system, affectionately known to Dubliners as DART, taking in the magnificent sweep of Dublin's horseshoe-shaped Bay. Afterwards enjoy a tour of North County Dublin. In the evening dinner at the superb Restaurant na Mara (Restaurant of the Sea) before attending a performance at Dublin's famous Abbey Theater.

**DAY 9—SUNDAY: Mysterious Newgrange and Stately Townley Hall**
Your first visit today is the site of one of Europe's great archaeological mysteries— Newgrange Neolithic Burial Tomb, which pre-dates even the Pyramids. Our next stop is nearby stately Townley Hall, a fine 18th century Georgian House, where you'll enjoy a guided tour followed by a light lunch. Roads once trodden by the Kings of Tara bear you northwards, across the River Foyle and into County Donegal and Letterkenny.

**DAY 10—MONDAY: Grand Atlantic Drive**
The Atlantic air here in the far north-west will put an edge on your appetite which even so, will be no match for a Donegal country breakfast. Come with us

Killiney Bay, Co. Dublin, a scenic view on your guided tour (Day 8).

today along the thrilling island-studded Atlantic coast, and in the afternoon a special visit to Glenveagh National Park, a wildlife sanctuary, preserved for the nation. You'll visit Glenveagh Castle, a castellated mansion surrounded by exotic gardens.

### DAY 11—TUESDAY: Yeats Country & Galway Bay
Our route this morning takes us to Sligo and tiny Drumcliffe Churchyard, the grave of the poet W.B. Yeats with its simple inscription: "Cast a cold eye on life, on death, horseman pass by". Continuing southwards through County Mayo and to the world famous pilgrimage village of Knock. Then to Galway for overnight.

### DAY 12—WEDNESDAY: Tour of Connemara
Today we have a full day trip through the starkly beautiful land of Connemara. You can almost feel the stillness as we travel through a fascinating area of contrasts from tiny rock-walled fields, sprinkled with sparkling lakes and rivers, to high purple-topped mountains. Your tour includes a visit to picturesque Kylemore Abbey on its lakeside setting. This evening, a sumptuous mediaeval banquet with entertainment in 16th century Dunguaire Castle.

### DAY 13—THURSDAY: Homeward Bound
Today we must bid farewells. After a hearty Irish breakfast, your coach takes you to Shannon Airport prior to the departure of the principal transatlantic flights.

**HOTELS:**
You will stay at the following hotels (or hotels of a similar standard):
**Shannonside:** Clare Inn (1 night)
**Killarney:** Great Southern Hotel (2 nights)
**Kilkenny:** Hotel Kilkenny (1 night)
**Dublin:** Burlington Hotel (3 nights)
**Letterkenny:** Mount Errigal Hotel (2 nights)
**Galway:** Corrib Great Southern Hotel (2 nights)

**NOTE:** Departure **July 20** will operate the tour itinerary in the reverse direction from Day 3 after breakfast.

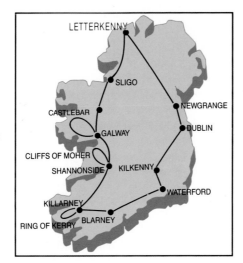

### YOUR PRICE INCLUDES:
* ★ **Round trip flight** from U.S. to Shannon by Aer Lingus flight, with dinner & continental breakfast on board.
* ★ **Sightseeing by luxury coach** throughout the tour.
* ★ **Professional Irish Driver/Guide** to escort and entertain you.
* ★ **Superior first class hotels** in rooms with private bath or shower for 11 nights.
* ★ **Full Irish breakfast daily** (except on day of arrival).
* ★ **Table d'hote dinner** each evening (except Day 7)
* ★ **Irish Ceili** dinner with country dances, singing and music.
* ★ **Mediaeval Banquet** at Dunguaire Castle.
* ★ **Dinner** at Ireland's leading seafood restaurant—Restaurant na Mara.
* ★ **Dinner at the Abbey Tavern** with traditional Irish music and song.
* ★ **Light lunch** at stately Townley Hall.
* ★ **Reserved Seats** at the Abbey Theater.
* ★ **A Guided Tour** on Dublin's ultra modern DART rail system taking in Dublin Bay.
* ★ **Tea and Scones** at an Irish Farmhouse.
* ★ **Jaunting car** tour in Killarney.
* ★ **Visits and admissions** to Muckross House Folk Museum, Blarney Castle, Blarney Woollen Mills, Waterford Crystal Showrooms, Kilkenny Castle, 6th century Glendalough, St. Patrick's Cathedral, Newgrange Neolithic Burial Tomb, stately Townley Hall, Glenveagh Castle and National Park, Royal Tara China Factory, Galway Cathedral and Kylemore Abbey.
* ★ **Tips** for baggage handling and to hotel personnel and all local taxes.
* ★ **Deluxe flight bag,** ticket wallet and luggage tags.

**IRISH TRADITION TOUR, CBCT    IT 1 EI 19102**
**DEPARTURE DATES EX. U.S.A. SATURDAYS: APRIL 27 THRU OCT. 12**

| PRICE PER PERSON SHARING ($US) | LAND COST | INCL. AIR JFK/BOS. | INCL. AIR CHICAGO |
|---|---|---|---|
| Apr. 27—May 11 | $1339 | $1906 | $1969 |
| May 18 | 1369 | 1936 | 1999 |
| May 25—June 08 | 1449 | 2016 | 2079 |
| June 15—Aug. 31 | 1449 | 2138 | 2147 |
| Sept. 07—Sept. 21 | 1449 | 2016 | 2079 |
| Sept. 28—Oct. 12 | 1339 | 1906 | 1969 |

**Single Room Supplement $299. Inclusive Air/Land** prices are based on Aer Lingus non-refundable APEX Fares (see conditions). **Standard APEX Fares** available on request. **Note:** Land only departures commence Day 2 Shannon Airport, Ireland. **"55 'N Smiling" Discounts:** $100 per person discounts apply to persons over 55 years on the following departures: Apr. 27; May 18; June 15; July 6; Aug. 3, 31; Sept. 14, 28; Oct. 5. Dept. Tax add $16.   *Page 11*

# IRISH ADVENTURE

**A great value tour designed for the budget traveler. 9 or 10 Day Vacation ★ ★ ★
FROM—$599**

**YOUR ITINERARY:**

**Day 1: Depart U.S for Dublin, Ireland**
Welcome aboard your Aer Lingus flight to Dublin. Dinner and continental breakfast on board.

**Day 2: Dublin's Fair City**
On arrival your driver will meet you and transfer you through Dublin City to the Montrose Hotel. The remainder of the day is yours to relax and shop in Dublin's many fashionable stores.

**Day 3: The Garden of Ireland**
This morning, you'll have a short Dublin City sightseeing tour before leaving Dublin, through the spectacular Wicklow Mountains to the tranquility of Glendalough. St. Kevin taught here in this 6th Century monastic settlement. Then to Waterford - the "Crystal City".

**Day 4: Blarney and Lakes of Killarney**
This morning, you'll visit the Waterford Crystal showrooms and then a special treat - tea and scones in an Irish Farmhouse. On to Blarney, where you can gain the "Gift of Eloquence" by kissing the famous Blarney Stone. Then over the mountains to Killarney's Lakes and Fells.

**Day 5: The Ring of Kerry Tour**
It was a poet who named this area "Heavens Reflex" but, as you'll see for yourself, even he couldn't quite capture the beauty which surrounds you as you travel in a long, lazy circle around the Iveragh Peninsula, known as the "Ring of Kerry". Spectacular views appear with every bend in the road and throughout the day.

**Day 6: Majestic Cliffs of Moher and Galway Bay**
Passing Tralee, you hear the sad romantic story of "The Rose of Tralee". Shortly afterwards board the Tarbert Ferry to cross the River Shannon. Along the coast of County Clare to the great Cliffs of Moher. You'll soon reach Galway. "City of the Tribes" - on its famous bay, then to Connemara for overnight.

**Day 7: Connemara and Yeats Country**
Your Connemara tour today, will take you through untamed natural beauty, a land of snug whitewashed mountain cottages, contrasting the misty-blue mountains. Along the way, see where the poet W.B. Yeats lies buried in the tiny Drumcliffe Churchyard. Overnight Sligo.

**Day 8: Mysterious Newgrange**
Today you'll travel to the site of one of Europe's great archaelogical mysteries - the tomb at Newgrange. A short drive takes you from the neolithic to the modern as your coach takes you to Dublin where you have the evening free.

**Day 9: Dublin**
Today we say farewell to passengers on Tour BAFT, who will be taken to Dublin Airport to connect with their transatlantic flights. Passengers on Tour BAJT will have today free to enjoy the sights and sounds of Dublin. These passengers will stay overnight in Dublin (Montrose Hotel) and after breakfast on Day 10 will have taxi transfers to Dublin Airport pre-arranged by CIE Tours.

**HOTELS:** You will stay at the following hotels (or hotels of a similar standard):

**Dublin:** Montrose Hotel (1 night)
**Waterford:** Dooley's Hotel (1 night)
**Killarney:** Ross Hotel (2 nights)
**Saturday Departures:** Kenmare Bay Hotel (2 nights)
**Furbo:** Connemara Coast Hotel (1 night)
**Sligo:** Sligo Park Hotel (1 night)
**Dublin:** Montrose Hotel (1 night-BAFT, 2 nights-BAJT)

**YOUR PRICE INCLUDES:**
★ **Round trip flight** from U.S. to Dublin by Aer Lingus, with dinner & continental breakfast on board.
★ **Sightseeing by luxury coach.**
★ **Superior hotels** with private bath or shower for 7 or 8 nights.
★ **Professional Irish Driver/Guide** to escort & entertain you.
★ **Full Irish breakfast daily** (except on day of arrival).
★ **Table d'hote dinner** each evening (except in Dublin).
★ **Tea & Scones** at an Irish Farmhouse.
★ **Visits & admissions** to 6th century Glendalough, Waterford Glass Factory (when open), Newgrange Neolithic Burial Tomb, Celtic Crystal Showrooms, Blarney Castle & Blarney Woollen Mills.
★ **Tips** for baggage handling and to hotel personnel.
★ **All local taxes.**

IRISH ADVENTURE TOUR BAFT (8 Day)   IT 1 EI 19124
**DEPARTURE DATES EX. U.S.A. FRIDAYS:** April 05 thru Oct. 25; **TUESDAYS:** April 30 thru Sept. 24;
**SATURDAYS:** June 08, 22; July 06, 20; Aug. 03, 17; Sept. 07, 21

| PRICE PER PERSON SHARING ($US) | LAND COST | INCL. AIR JFK/BOS | INCL. AIR CHICAGO |
|---|---|---|---|
| April 05—April 30 | $599 | $1196 | $1259 |
| May 03—May 31 | 639 | 1236 | 1299 |
| June 04—June 14 | 719 | 1316 | 1379 |
| June 18—Aug 30 | 719 | 1424 | 1424 |
| Sept. 03—Sept. 27 | 719 | 1316 | 1379 |
| Oct. 04—Oct. 25 | 639 | 1236 | 1279 |

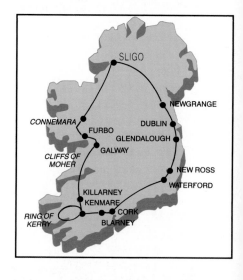

**Tour BAJT** (9 Day Vacation) IT 1 EI 12437, add $75 to above prices. **Single room supplements:** Tour BAFT $199, Tour BAJT $225. **Inclusive Air/Land prices** are based on Aer Lingus non-refundable APEX Fares (see conditions). **Weekend surcharges** of $14 JFK/BOS and $23 Chicago apply each way between June 15—Aug. 31. **Standard APEX Fares** available on request. **Note:** Land only departures commence Day 2 Dublin Airport. Ireland.

# TASTE OF IRELAND

## Highlights of the Emerald Isle
## 4, 5 or 7 Day Vacation ★ ★ ★ ★

We won't claim that you can get to know the whole of Ireland in just 5 days - but we do promise you the highlights: Dublin, Shannonside, Killarney, Blarney, Waterford - you'll see them all. In Dublin you'll visit Christ Church Cathedral and join the revelry and song at an Irish Cabaret. You'll dine like a lord at an elegant Mediaeval Banquet in an authentic Irish Castle, you'll kiss the Blarney Stone, and you'll stay at first class hotels.

**YOUR ITINERARY:**

**DAY 1—FRIDAY: To Dublin's Fair City**
Welcome to Dublin's Fair and Friendly City. Your tour begins in the afternoon with a sightseeing trip around this exciting capital. You'll visit Christ Church Cathedral before returning to your hotel and have time to relax before tonight's fun-filled cabaret and dinner.

**DAY 2—SATURDAY: Mediaeval Majesty**
Away through Ireland's striking green countryside today. You'll soon reach historic Limerick City - then to Shannonside where tonight you'll enjoy a banquet in a 15th century Mediaeval Castle.

**DAY 3—SUNDAY: Lakes of Killarney**
Today your first stop will be in Adare, one of Ireland's prettiest villages. On to Killarney with its famous mountain shadowed lakes, its forests and its glens. Sit back and enjoy it all from your Irish Jaunting Car - a delightful trip. Time for shopping in Killarney.

**DAY 4—MONDAY: Blarney Castle & Waterford**
Leaving Killarney this morning our road meanders along by the River Lee to Blarney. You can gain the "Gift of Eloquence" here and visit the shopping treasure house of Blarney Woollen Mills. On to Waterford - home of the beautiful crystal - we'll visit the crystal factory when open.

**DAY 5—TUESDAY: The Garden of Ireland**
Today we travel through Co. Wicklow, known as the Garden of Ireland - we'll visit the 6th century Monastic Settlement at Glendalough, from where we continue to Dublin. For passengers on **Tour BGFT,** their Taste of Ireland concludes at the Central Bus Station, Dublin 17.00 Hours approx.
**Tour BGJT** passengers will continue to Burlington Hotel where they will be based for nights 5 (Tuesday) and 6 (Wednesday). They will be at leisure to explore Dublin on their own. Taxi transfers to Dublin Airport on Day 7 (Thursday) will be arranged by CIE Tours.
**Hotels:** The following hotels (or hotels of similar standard) will be used:
**Dublin:** Burlington Hotel (1 night)
**Shannonside:** Shannon Great Southern (1 night)
**Killarney:** Royal Hotel (1 night)
**Waterford:** Tower Hotel (1 night)
**Dublin:** Burlington Hotel (2 nights-BGJT only)

*Treated like royalty at an elegant Mediaeval Banquet in an Irish Castle (Day 2).*

**YOUR PRICE INCLUDES:**
★ **Round trip flight** from U.S. to Dublin by Aer Lingus with dinner & continental breakfast on board—only passengers taking Tour BGJT may avail of incl. Air/Land Program.
★ **Sightseeing by luxury coach** throughout your tour.
★ **First-class hotels** in rooms w/private bath or shower
★ **Professional Irish Driver/Guide** to escort and entertain you.
★ **Full Irish breakfast daily.**
★ **Irish Cabaret** & dinner in Dublin (Day 1).
★ **Mediaeval Banquet** in an Irish Castle (Day 2).
★ **Table d'hote dinner** - Days 3 & 4.
★ **Visit and admission** to Christ Church Cathedral, Dublin, Blarney Castle, Blarney Woollen Mills, & 6th century Glendalough.
★ **Tips** for baggage handling & to hotel personnel.
★ **All Local Taxes.**

---

**4 DAY TOUR OPTIONS—**
**Starting in Dublin:** If you prefer, you may join the "Taste of Ireland" tour for 4 days starting from the Burlington Hotel, Dublin at 08.30 hours on Day 2. **Please ask for Tour BGBT.**
**OR Starting at Shannon:** You may also take the tour from Shannon by joining at the Shannon Great Southern Hotel, Shannon Airport, at 14.30 hours on Day 2. **Please ask for Tour BGCT.**
Both 4 day tours conclude at the Central Bus Station, Dublin, at 17.00 hours (approximately) on Day 5
**PRICES:** MAY -$ 425.00,
June thru Sept. -$ 465.00
Single Room Supplement: $98.00

THE TASTE OF IRELAND    IT 1 EI 12438
DEPARTURE DATES EX. DUBLIN 5 Day Tour BGFT: Fridays May 10 thru Sept. 27.
DEPARTURE DATES EX. DUBLIN 7 Day Tour BGJT: Fridays May 10 thru Sept. 27.
PRICE PER PERSON SHARING ($US)

| SEASON | Tour BGFT 5 Day Land | Tour BGJT 7 Day Land | Tour BGJT Incl.Air JFK/BOS | Tour BGJT Incl.Air CHICAGO |
|---|---|---|---|---|
| May 10—May 31 | $585 | $775 | $1372 | $1435 |
| June 07—June 14 | 635 | 839 | 1436 | 1499 |
| June 21—Aug. 30 | 635 | 839 | 1544 | 1544 |
| Sept. 06—Sept. 27 | 635 | 839 | 1436 | 1499 |

**Single room supplements:** Tour BGFT $130; Tour BGJT $195.
**Inclusive Air/Land** prices for the 7 day BGJT Tour are based on Aer Lingus non-refundable APEX Fares (see conditions). **Standard APEX Fares** available on request. The departure day ex. U.S.A. for BGJT is Thursdays. Persons booking the land tours join their coach at 2:00 p.m. Fridays at the Burlington Hotel.

# IRISH WELCOME

**A unique opportunity to meet the Irish at home on this friendly tour**
**11 Days Vacation ★ ★ ★**
**FROM—$869      "55 'N SMILING" FROM—$794**

On this tour you'll become part of an Irish family and experience the unique hospitality for which the Irish are famous. As you travel around the scenic countryside of Kerry, Donegal and Galway, you'll be welcomed into "town and country homes". In Dublin and Shannonside you'll overnight in first class hotels. Each day you'll explore the scenic highlights of the area with your professional Irish driver/guide. In the evenings, dine family-style, sit by the open fireplace, chat or join in a "singsong". You'll enjoy the best of Irish country cuisine - from farmgrown produce, home-baked scones and brown bread to traditional dishes like Irish stew.

**YOUR ITINERARY:**
**DAY 1-FRIDAY: Depart U.S. for Shannon, Ireland**
Welcome aboard your Aer Lingus flight to Shannon. Dinner and continental breakfast on board.
**DAY 2—SATURDAY: Arrival Shannonside -Irish Ceili**
The tour starts at Shannon Airport with a transfer to your hotel. The afternoon is free to relax before you'll attend tonight's traditional dinner and Irish Ceili in Bunratty Folk Park with a rousing evening of country dances, singing and music.
**DAY 3—SUNDAY: Majestic Cliffs of Moher**
Start off this morning with a tour to the mighty Cliffs of Moher, a sheer 700 feet above the sea. Then southwards through historic Limerick City and the picturesque village of Adare, before reaching lovely Killarney, and your Irish family hosts for the next two nights.
**DAY 4—MONDAY: The Ring of Kerry Tour**
Your day begins as you skirt the shoulders of Ireland's highest mountains, the MacGillycuddy Reeks, to begin a journey through 100 miles of breathtaking vistas which follow one after the other at every turn of this spectacular winding coast road. Then back to Killarney by the lush lakeside.

**DAY 5—TUESDAY: The Blarney Stone**
Leaving Killarney this morning you'll travel to Blarney. Here you'll win the "gift of Irish eloquence", by kissing the magical Blarney Stone. You'll visit Blarney Woollen Mills before travelling to Cork City, and continuing through the Golden Vale, you'll soon reach Dublin where you'll have the evening free. Overnight Tara Tower Hotel.
**DAY 6—WEDNESDAY: Dublin's Fair City**
This morning's sightseeing tour of Dublin will show you this elegant, artistic city - from the Georgian Squares and buildings to the imposing grandeur of St. Patrick's Cathedral. The afternoon in this friendly city is free for shopping. Later this evening there is an optional trip at extra cost to The Abbey Tavern for dinner, traditional Irish music and song.
**DAY 7—THURSDAY: Stately Carrigglas Manor**
Leaving Dublin this morning, you'll visit Carrigglas Manor, one of Ireland's most beautiful stately homes, in County Longford. Then northwest through the glens and mountain passes of County Donegal before reaching Ballyshannon, where you'll stay in family homes for the next two nights.
**DAY 8—FRIDAY: Hills of Donegal Tour**
A long beautiful coastline, majestic mountains, deep glens and shimmering lakes merge in a tumult of beauty. Today you'll savor them all - as you tour through Glenties and by the Blue Stack range. You'll visit magnificent Glenveagh Castle and National Park before returning to Ballyshannon.

**DAY 9—SATURDAY: Yeats Country and Galway Bay**
Our drive today takes you through "Yeats Country" of County Sligo and to see the little churchyard where the poet was buried. Continuing southwards through County Mayo and to the world famous pilgrimage village of Knock. You'll soon reach Galway, "City of the Tribes" - on its famous bay, and your Irish family home for the next two nights.
**DAY 10—SUNDAY: Tour of Connemara**
Today we take the round trip journey through the starkly beautiful land of Connemara. You can almost feel the stillness while you travel through a land of misty blue mountains, small stone-walled fields and tiny lily-covered lakes, and where native Irish is still the spoken language. Your tour includes a visit to lakeside Kylemore Abbey and the Celtic Crystal Showrooms. This evening a sumptuous Mediaeval Banquet at Dunguaire Castle.
**DAY 11—MONDAY: Homeward Bound**
Sadly today, we must say "Slan Leat" farewell. Our coach will bring you to Shannon in plenty of time for last minute duty free shopping at the extensively stocked Shannon Airport.
**Your Accommodation:**
**Shannonside:** West County Hotel (1 night)
**Killarney:** Town & Country Homes (2 nights)
**Dublin:** Tara Tower Hotel (2 nights)
**Ballyshannon:** Town & Country Homes (2 nights)
**Galway:** Town & Country Homes (2 nights)

*A friendly Irish Welcome awaits you.*

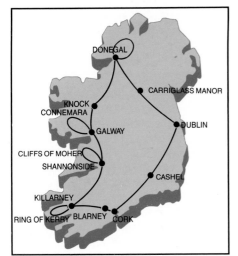

# "55 'N SMILING" DISCOUNTS

*Stately Carrigglas Manor, Co. Longford · your visit on Day 7.*

*Magical Blarney Castle · visit on Day 5.*

*Celtic Crystal.*

**YOUR PRICE INCLUDES:**

★ **Round trip flight** from U.S to Shannon by Aer Lingus flight, with dinner and continental breakfast on board.

★ **Sightseeing by luxury coach** throughout the tour.

★ **9 nights accommodation** (3 nights in hotels with private bath or shower and 6 nights in Irish family homes).

★ **Professional Irish Driver/Guide** to escort and entertain you.

★ **Full Irish breakfast daily** (except on day of arrival).

★ **Dinner** each evening except in Dublin.

★ **Mediaeval Banquet** and entertainment at Dunguaine Castle.

★ **Irish Ceili** with traditional dinner, music, song and dancing.

★ **Tea and Scones** at an Irish Farmhouse.

★ **Visits and admissions** to Blarney Castle, Blarney Woollen Mills, Carrigglas Manor, St. Patrick's Cathedral, Dublin, Glenveagh Castle and National Park, Kylemore Abbey, Celtic Crystal Showrooms and Galway Cathedral.

★ **Tips** for baggage handling and to hotel personnel.

★ **All Local Taxes.**

IRISH WELCOME TOUR BPBT   IT 1 El 19101
DEPARTURE DATES EX. U.S.A. FRIDAYS MAY 17 THRU SEPT. 20
PRICE PER PERSON SHARING ($US)

|  | LAND COST | INCL. AIR JFK/BOS | INCL. AIR CHICAGO |
|---|---|---|---|
| May 17—June 14 | $869 | $1436 | $1499 |
| June 21—Aug. 30 | 869 | 1558 | 1567 |
| Sept. 06—Sept. 20 | 869 | 1436 | 1499 |

**Single room supplement:** $175. **Inclusive Air/Land** prices are based on Aer Lingus non-refundable APEX Fares (see conditions). **Standard APEX Fares** available on request.
**"55 'N Smiling" Discounts:** $75 per person discounts apply to persons over 55 years on the following departures: May 24; June 21, 28; July 12; August 9, 30; Sept. 20.
NOTE: Land only departures commence Day 2 Shannon Airport, Ireland.

# THE FOUR PROVINCES

## 12 Day Vacation ★ ★ ★     FROM—$1124     "55 'N SMILING" FROM—$1024

### Explore the beauty and variety of the four corners of Ireland

"Where the mountains of Mourne sweep down to the sea . . ." in the north east, Kerry, in the south west, where the rugged headlands stretch into the Atlantic Ocean, the "Green Glens of Antrim" in the north east, and all the way back to Dublin on the east coast. You'll explore the beauty of Connemara, the majestic Cliffs of Moher and the extraordinary phenomenon of Giants Causeway. A truly memorable vacation.

**YOUR ITINERARY:**

**DAY 1—THURSDAY: Depart U.S. for Shannon, Ireland**
Welcome aboard your Aer Lingus flight to Shannon. Dinner and continental breakfast on board.

**DAY 2—FRIDAY: Arrival Shannonside · Mediaeval Splendour**
The tour starts at Shannon Airport. You overnight in the Shannon Shamrock Hotel (or Clare Inn Hotel) eight miles away in the green heart of Ireland. This evening, after a restful day, enjoy a sumptuous Medieval Banquet in a 15th century Irish Castle.

**DAY 3—SATURDAY: Majestic Cliffs of Moher & Lakes of Killarney**
Your day begins with a trip to the mighty Cliffs of Moher, 700 feet over the pounding Atlantic waves. Then travel southwards along the coast of County Clare to the Killimer Ferry to cross the River Shannon, before continuing to Killarney's Lakes and Fells.

**DAY 4—SUNDAY: The Ring of Kerry**
The "Ring of Kerry" drive takes you around the beautiful Iveragh Peninsula. A round trip of over 100 miles, with changing views of seascapes and mountain ranges at almost every turn.

**DAY 5—MONDAY: Blarney Castle & Waterford's Crystal City**
Travel eastwards today, to Blarney, where you'll acquire the "gift of eloquence" by kissing the famous stone. Time to visit the Blarney Woollen Mills before continuing to Waterford, famous for its crystal.

**DAY 6—TUESDAY: The Garden of Ireland · Dublin**
This morning we visit the Waterford Crystal Showrooms, before traveling through Wicklow "the Garden of Ireland" to Glendalough and its 6th century monastic settlement. Your tour continues to Dublin, where this evening at an optional cost you

may wish to attend the lively Doyles Irish Cabaret Show.

**DAY 7—WEDNESDAY: Dublin's Fair City**
This morning's sightseeing tour of Dublin, will show you this elegant, artistic city. The afternoon is yours to browse and shop. Tonight an optional trip (at extra cost) to the renowned Abbey Tavern in Howth for dinner and music session.

**DAY 8—THURSDAY: Mysterious Newgrange & The Mountains of Mourne**
Our first stop today is at the Neolithic tombs at Newgrange, which pre-date even the Pyramids. Continue to Newry and the magnificent Mountains of Mourne. Then to Kilbroney County House Hotel, just outside the charming village of Rostrevor.

**DAY 9—FRIDAY: Green Glens of Antrim & Giant's Causeway**
Your tour today takes you first to Downpatrick where St. Patrick is believed to have been buried. Then through the "Green Glens of Antrim". Next we see the extraordinary coastal rock phenomenon, Giant's Causeway, before continuing to the historic Derry for overnight.

**DAY 10—SATURDAY: Fermanagh Lake Country & Yeats Country**
Traveling south through Fermanagh Lake Country to Sligo and tiny Drumcliffe Churchyard, the grave of the poet W.B. Yeats. Continue through County Mayo to Knock, the major pilgrimage centre. On to the Galway area for overnight.

THE FOUR PROVINCES TOUR CCFT
IT 1 EI 12439
Dept.Dates & Prices
Depart U.S.A.
Thursdays

|         | Land  | Incl.Air JFK/Bos | Incl.Air Chicago |
|---------|-------|------------------|------------------|
| May 30  | $1124 | $1691            | $1754            |
| June 13 | 1124  | 1691             | 1754             |
| July 11 | 1124  | 1799             | 1799             |
| July 25 | 1124  | 1799             | 1799             |
| Aug 08  | 1124  | 1799             | 1799             |
| Aug 15  | 1124  | 1799             | 1799             |
| Sept 05 | 1124  | 1691             | 1754             |
| Sept 19 | 1124  | 1691             | 1754             |

Single Room Supplement $289. Inclusive Air/Land prices are based on Aer Lingus non-refundable APEX Fares (see conditions). Standard APEX Fares available on request. NOTE: Land tours commence Day 2 Shannon Airport. Ireland. "55 'N Smiling" Discounts: $100 per person discounts apply to persons over 55 years on the following departures: May 30. July 25. Aug. 15 & Sept. 19.

**DAY 11—SUNDAY: Galway Bay & Connemara Tour**
Our tour today takes us along the shores of Galway Bay and further west into Connemara, a land of untamed natural beauty. Visit lakeside Kylemore Abbey and the Celtic Crystal showrooms.

**DAY 12—MONDAY: Homeward Bound · Departure Shannon**
Sadly today, we must say "Slan Leat" farewell. Our coach will bring you to Shannon where you'll check in for your Aer Lingus transatlantic flight. You'll have plenty of time for duty-free shopping in the world's first duty-free shop.

**YOUR PRICE INCLUDES:**
- ★ **Round trip flight** from U.S. to Shannon by Aer Lingus with dinner and continental breakfast on board.
- ★ **Sightseeing** by luxury motorcoach throughout your tour.
- ★ **Superior hotels** with private bath or shower for 10 nights.
- ★ **Professional Driver/Guide** to escort and entertain you.
- ★ **Full Irish breakfast daily** (except on day of arrival).
- ★ **Table d'hote dinner** each evening (except in Dublin).
- ★ **Visits and admissions** to Blarney Castle, Blarney Woollen Mills, Waterford Glass Showrooms (when open), 6th century Glendalough, St. Patrick's Cathedral, Newgrange Neolitic Burial Tomb, Giants Causeway, Galway Cathedral, Celtic Crystal Showrooms and Kylemore Abbey.
- ★ **Mediaeval Banquet** at a 15th century Irish Castle.
- ★ **Tips** for baggage handling and to local personnel.
- ★ **All local taxes.**

**HOTELS:** The following Hotels or hotels of a similar standard will be used:
**Shannonside:** Shannon Shamrock or Clare Inn (1 night)
**Killarney:** International Hotel (2 nights)
**Waterford:** Tower Hotel (1 night)
**Dublin:** Montrose Hotel (2 nights)
**Rostrevor:** Kilbroney Country House (1 night)
**Derry:** Everglades Hotel (1 night)
**Galway:** Connemara Gateway/Coast or Corrib Great Southern (2 nights)

# DUBLIN'S FAIR CITY

## Stay 3 days or longer in Ireland's friendly capital

DUBLIN 1991
EUROPEAN CITY of CULTURE

Dublin, selected as European City of Culture for 1991, will celebrate this honor with a non-stop program covering all aspects of Dublin's history, culture, arts and entertainment. Festivals of music, literature, theatre & heritage will be highlights but Dublin's history is written in its streets and buildings from the Viking settlements by the River Liffey to Trinity College and the Book of Kells. Joyce, Yeats, Shaw, Wilde, Behan & O'Casey walked its streets and were inspired. Downtown Dublin has a number of pedestrianized streets giving the shopping areas of Grafton St. and Henry St. a festive air where you are likely to come across buskers dressed in evening wear playing Chopin's Nocturne or a mime artist captivating his audience with impressions of daily life.

With your Dublin Explorer Pass you have unlimited travel by bus and commuter rail for 4 days. You'll visit "The Dublin Experience" in Trinity College, a brief but fascinating look at Dublin life through the ages. A ticket to one of Dublin's famous theatres and the Dublin Heritage Trail city tour by open deck bus will be included in your program.

*The River Liffey in the heart of Dublin*

**Even greater VALUE with two perfect combinations that save you money!**
Why not combine this Dublin vacation program with one of our Irish Selfdrive programs shown on pages 4 & 5. On the other hand you can take a Selfdrive tour, and opt for accommodation only in Dublin without the extra features. See applicable extra nights rate in table below.

*A Break in the Countryside.*

**YOUR PRICE INCLUDES:**
★ **Accommodation for 3 nights** or more at your choice of first class or deluxe hotels in rooms with private bath or shower.
★ **Full Irish breakfast daily.**
★ **Round trip transfers** between Dublin Airport & your hotel (by taxi).
★ **Dublin Heritage Trail City Tour** by open deck bus.
★ **Theater ticket** to one of Dublin's famous Theaters.
★ **Visit** to "The Dublin Experience" in Trinity College (May 20—Oct. 2 only)
★ **Free four-day** Dublin Explorer Bus and Rail Pass (which includes discounts on shopping, sightseeing tours and meals.
★ **Services** of our Dublin office for on-the-spot assistance.
★ **Hotel service charges.**
★ **All local taxes.**

3 NIGHT VACATION—(minimum stay)     LAND PRICES PER PERSON                                      TOUR FKDB

| Hotels | Grade | Jan—Apr | | May & Oct | | June—Sept | | Nov & Dec | |
|---|---|---|---|---|---|---|---|---|---|
| | | Three Nights | Extra Nights | Three Nights | Extra Nights | Three Nights | Extra Nights | Three Nights | Extra Nights |
| Montrose | 1st Class | $209 | $40 | $275 | $59 | $299 | $66 | $247 | $48 |
| Tara Tower | 1st Class | 209 | 40 | 275 | 59 | 299 | 66 | 247 | 48 |
| Skylon | 1st Class | 209 | 40 | 275 | 59 | 299 | 66 | 247 | 48 |
| Mont Clare | Superior | 303 | 74 | 318 | 77 | 348 | 85 | 303 | 74 |
| Burlington | Superior | 252 | 54 | 329 | 76 | 355 | 85 | 292 | 64 |
| Westbury | Deluxe | 419 | 112 | 433 | 115 | 458 | 122 | 419 | 112 |
| Berkeley Court | Deluxe | 419 | 112 | 433 | 115 | 458 | 122 | 419 | 112 |

**Single room supplement per night:** Montrose/Skylon/Tara Tower—$23; Mont Clare—$40; Burlington—$30; Westbury/Berkeley Court—$50.

# LONDON ROYAL SPLENDOR

**Stay 3 days or longer in Europe's most exciting city.**

London, with its royal pageantry and splendor - from Buckingham Palace and the Changing of the Guard to the Tower of London where the fabulous Crown Jewels are displayed; from attractions like Westminster Abbey, Houses of Parliment, Big Ben to Piccadilly Circus and the famous West End, with its many chic shops, restaurants, theaters and exciting nightlife. We'll provide you with a 4 day "London Travel Card" which gives you unlimited travel on London's famous red buses and underground rail system; a Theater pass for one of London's top shows with up to 25 to choose from; and a free city sightseeing tour.

## Even greater VALUE with two perfect combinations that save you money!

Why not combine this London vacation program with one of our Selfdrive programs shown on pages 20/21.

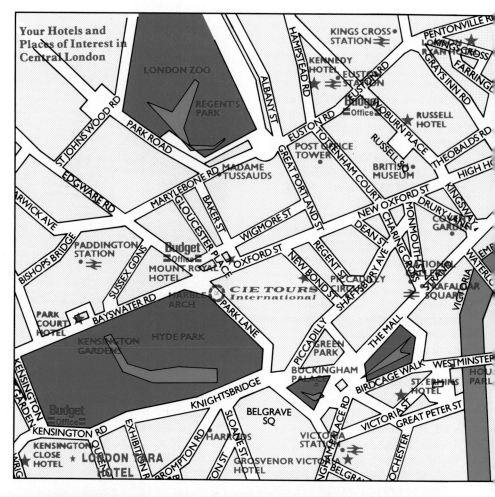

*Trooping the Color at Buckingham Palace.*

**LONDON RYAN HOTEL:** Modern 3 star hotel near Kings Cross Station and close to British Museum. Restaurant, coffee shop and bar. Rooms with color TV, direct-dial phone, in-house movies and radio/alarm.

**KENNEDY HOTEL:** Modern 3 star hotel close to Euston Station. Near Madame Tussauds, Regents Park and Post Office Tower. Restaurant and bar. Rooms with color TV, direct-dial phone and radio.

**PARK COURT HOTEL:** Recently refurbished 3 star hotel overlooking Hyde Park and Kensington Gardens. Not far from Oxford street, Mayfair and West End. Rooms with color TV, radio, direct-dial phone, tea/coffee making facilities. Restaurant, bar and coffee shop.

**MOUNT ROYAL HOTEL:** Large 3 star hotel in excellent location on Oxford Street, a few minutes walk from Marble Arch and Hyde Park. Restaurant, coffee shop, bar, beauty salon, gift shop. Rooms with color TV, direct-dial phone, radio and tea/coffee making facilities.

**GROSVENOR VICTORIA HOTEL:** Recently renovated 4 star hotel adjacent to Victoria Station. Near Buckingham Palace and Houses of Parliament. Restaurant and lounges. Rooms with color TV, phone.

**KENSINGTON CLOSE HOTEL:** A 4 star hotel located minutes away from Kensington's fashionable High Street. Restaurant, bar, indoor swimming pool, squash courts, sauna and gymnasium. Rooms with color TV, radio and phone.

**RUSSELL HOTEL:** A superb example of Victorian architecture, this 4 star hotel overlooks Russell Square and is near the British Museum. Restaurant, bar, rooms with color TV, radio and direct-dial phone.

**ST. ERMINS HOTEL:** A 4 star hotel located in the heart of Westminster and only a short walk from Buckingham Palace and Westminster Abbey. Two restaurants and a cocktail bar. Rooms with color TV, phone, tea/coffee making facilities, hair-dryer, trouser press and a daily fresh bowl of fruit.

**LONDON TARA:** Modern 4 star hotel in fashionable area near High Street, Kensington Tube Station, Kensington Garden and Hyde Park. Restaurants, 2 bars and 24 hour room service. Rooms temperature controlled, with color TV, direct-dial phone, in-house movies and tea/coffee making facilities.

*Kennedy Hotel*

## YOUR PRICE INCLUDES:

★ **Choice of First Class or Deluxe Hotels** for 3 nights or more in rooms with private bath or shower.

★ **Continental Breakfast Daily.**

★ **Round Trip Transfers** between Heathrow or Gatwick Airports and Central London by subway/rail.

★ **Four day "London Visitor Travelcard"** with unlimited transportation on London's famous red buses and extensive underground systems.

★ **Theater Pass** to be exchanged for one theater ticket from a wide selection of London's leading theaters.

★ **Free London Sightseeing Tour.**

★ **Hotel Service Charges.**

★ **All Local Taxes.**

Gatwick Transfers
on request only.

*Russel Hotel (The Carvery).*

*Kensington Close (The Restaurant)*

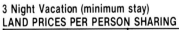

*St. Ermins Hotel.*

3 Night Vacation (minimum stay)
LAND PRICES PER PERSON SHARING                                    TOUR FKLB

| HOTELS | Jan thru Mar Nov thru Dec | | Apr thru Oct | |
|---|---|---|---|---|
|  | 3 nights | Extra nights | 3 nights | Extra nights |
| Kennedy | $299 | $68 | $348 | $84 |
| London Ryan | 294 | 65 | 336 | 80 |
| Mount Royal | 358 | 88 | 411 | 105 |
| Park Court | 309 | 71 | 369 | 89 |
| Grosvenor Victoria | 391 | 98 | 438 | 114 |
| Kensington Close | 343 | 82 | 394 | 99 |
| Russell | 399 | 102 | 492 | 132 |
| St. Ermins | 373 | 99 | 429 | 111 |
| London Tara | 385 | 96 | 425 | 110 |

**Single Room Supplement Per Night:** Kennedy $40; London Ryan $40; Mount Royal $45; Park Court $45; Grosvenor Victoria $50; Kensington Close $40; Russell $45; St. Ermins $45; London Tara $65.

# SELFDRIVE VACATIONS IN BRITAIN

## Hotels in England, Scotland and Wales

Value and variety are the keynotes of this flexible Go As You Please Hotel vacation of England, Scotland and Wales. We have made special arrangements for you with nearly 300 great hotels from the Consort Hotel Group.

From modern city-center hotels to historic coaching inns and stately country properties, each with its own distinctive character and charm, but all offering value for money and a warm friendly welcome.

And CIE Tours will make it all so easy. We will provide you with a current model car, vouchers to cover your hotel accommodation with bath or shower for each night including full breakfast daily (continental breakfast in London), map of Britain & accommodation list, so that you can design your own itinerary to the Britain of your choice. Each hotel will ensure you get every assistance to secure the hotel of your choice for your next nights stop - that's why we've selected Consort Hotels to be your hosts in Britain. We'll reserve on request your first night's accommodation, then away you go to find the Britain of your dreams.

### YOUR PRICE INCLUDES:

★ **Self Drive Car** Standard Shift Ford Fiesta (or similar Group "A" current model).
★ **Unlimited mileage and government tax (V.A.T.) on car rental.**
★ **Accommodation** for duration of your stay at choice of over 300 first class Consort Hotels in rooms with private bath or shower.
★ **Full Breakfast daily** (except continental breakfast in London).
★ **First night pre-booked** on request. CIE Tours will reserve free of charge your first nights accommodation in London at time of booking vacation only.
★ **Royal Automobile Club (RAC)** 24-hour emergency service.
★ **Free CIE Tours Exclusive "Touring through the Treasure Isles" audio tape** - a lively 60 minute program of travel hints (one per couple).
★ **FREE** touring map of Britain.
★ **Hotel service charges.**
★ **All local taxes.**
★ **Three persons** traveling together & occupying twin & single room throughout, will receive a standard shift Ford Escort (or similar group "B" rental car) at **no extra charge.**
★ **Four persons** traveling & booking two twin bedded rooms, will receive a standard-shift Ford Sierra (or similar group "C" rental car) at **no extra charge.**

*Newton Hotel, Nairn, Scotland*

### Even greater VALUE with two perfect combinations that save you money!

Why not combine any of the self-drive vacations on these 2 pages with our London program shown on pages 18/19 or opt for accommodation only in London without the extras.

---

**FREE EXTRA** . . . *on any of the tours on these two pages*
Before you even leave home, you'll receive your FREE personal copy of
*"TOURING THROUGH THE TREASURE ISLES" AUDIO TAPE*

---

Hotels—Land Prices per person                                                     TOUR PKLL

| No. of Per.traveling | Jan.—Apr. and Oct.—Dec. | | | May—Sept | | |
|---|---|---|---|---|---|---|
| | Three Nights | One Week (6 nights) | Extra Days | Three Nights | One Week (6 nights) | Extra Days |
| 4 | $231 | $441 | $70 | $253 | $487 | $78 |
| *3 | 233 | 443 | 70 | 259 | 493 | 78 |
| 2 | 236 | 449 | 71 | 262 | 499 | 79 |
| *1 | 288 | 540 | 84 | 324 | 606 | 94 |

*Single room supplement** not included and is payable directly to the hotel—£10.00 sterling per person per night. A few superior "Crown" hotels carry a supplement of £7.00 sterling per person per night and is payable in cash directly to the hotel. **Reduction** of $25 per night per child under 12 years sharing room with parents. ★ Supplements apply for larger or automatic cars. Details on request.
★ Government Tax (VAT) on Car Rental included in our prices.

# WITH HOTELS OR FARMHOUSES

## Farm & Country Homes in England, Scotland and Wales

*A Farmhouse in Wales*

Our British Heritage Farm and Country Homes vacation offers a blend of Britain's best - four star category - from mansions and manor homes to modern houses; thatched cottages to Cornish farmhouses, and Cotswold stone cottages to hunting lodges. You can choose from over 400 superb homes throughout England, Scotland and Wales.

### 4 STAR HOMES

If you'd like to spoil yourself, then this is the tour for you. You'll stay in homes with every modern comfort, and enjoy personal attention in a friendly and informal atmosphere. These superior homes reflect the best of both traditional and modern architecture - superbly maintained, superbly finished and all with excellent facilities. Some houses date back as far as the four-teenth century but each has been carefully chosen for its atmosphere, and friendly hospitality.

### YOUR PRICE INCLUDES:

* ★ **Self Drive Car** Standard Shift Ford Fiesta (or similar Group "A" current model).
* ★ **Unlimited mileage and government tax (V.A.T) on car rental.**
* ★ **Accommodation** for duration of your stay at a choice of Four Star Farm & Country Homes.
* ★ **Full Breakfast daily.**
* ★ **First night pre-booked** on request. CIE Tours will reserve free of charge your first nights accommodation at time of booking vacation only.
* ★ **Royal Automobile Club (RAC)** 24-hour emergency service.
* ★ **Free CIE Tours Exclusive "Touring through the Treasure Isles" audio tape** - a lively 60 minute program of travel hints (one per couple).
* ★ **FREE** touring map of Britain.
* ★ **All local taxes.**
* ★ **Three persons** traveling together & occupying twin & single room throughout will receive a standard-shift Ford Escort (or similar Group "B" rental car) at **no extra charge.**
* ★ **Four persons** traveling & booking two twin bedded rooms will receive a standard-shift Ford Sierra (or similar Group "C" rental car) at **no extra charge.**

*A typical British farm and country home.*

*See the wonders of Stonehenge*

4 Star Farmhouses—Land Prices per person                         TOUR PKNN

| No. of Per.traveling | Apr.and Oct. | | | May—Sept | | |
|---|---|---|---|---|---|---|
| | Three Nights | One Week (6 nights) | Extra Days | Three Nights | One Week (6 nights) | Extra Days |
| 4 | $222 | $420 | $66 | $223 | $427 | $68 |
| *3 | 222 | 423 | 67 | 229 | 433 | 68 |
| 2 | 225 | 429 | 68 | 232 | 439 | 69 |
| *1 | 281 | 527 | 82 | 292 | 544 | 84 |

*Single room supplement** not included and is payable directly to the hotel. ★ **Reduction of $16** per night per child under 12 years sharing room with parents. ★ **Supplements** apply for larger or automatic cars. Details on request. ★ **Government Tax (VAT) on Car Rental** included in our prices.

# CAR HIRE RATES

Ford Fiesta

Ford Orion

Ford Sierra

Granada Ghia

## IRELAND

**FANTASTIC VALUE CAR HIRE RATES**
* ★ UNLIMITED MILEAGE
* ★ ALL LOCAL TAXES—INCLUDING VAT.
* ★ USE A MAJOR CREDIT CARD AND AVOID C.D.W. PAYMENTS
  (see pages 4 & 5 for information)

| GROUP/CAR TYPE | JAN-APR OCT-DEC | | MAY-JUNE SEPT | | JULY-AUG | |
|---|---|---|---|---|---|---|
| | 7 Days $ | Extra Day $ | 7 Days $ | Extra Day $ | 7 Days $ | Extra Day $ |
| (A) Fiesta/Micra | 189 | 27 | 210 | 30 | 273 | 39 |
| (C) Orion/Sunny | 224 | 32 | 301 | 43 | 322 | 46 |
| (D) Sierra/Carina | 273 | 39 | 315 | 45 | 385 | 55 |
| (F) Micra Automatic | 294 | 42 | 385 | 55 | 448 | 64 |
| (G) Sunny Automatic | 336 | 48 | 427 | 61 | 497 | 71 |

## BRITAIN

* ★ UNLIMITED MILEAGE
* ★ ALL LOCAL TAXES INCLUDING V.A.T. AT 15%
* ★ ROYAL AUTOMOBILE CLUB (R.A.C.) 24 HOUR EMERGENCY SERVICE
* ★ WITH A MAJOR CREDIT CARD YOU MAY AVOID C.D.W. PAYMENTS
  (See pages 20 & 21 for information)

| GROUP/CAR TYPE | JAN-MAY OCT-DEC | | JUNE-SEPT | |
|---|---|---|---|---|
| | 7 Days $ | Extra Day $ | 7 Days $ | Extra Day $ |
| (A) Ford Fiesta | 189 | 27 | 203 | 29 |
| (B) Ford Escort | 273 | 39 | 287 | 41 |
| (C) Ford Sierra | 350 | 50 | 364 | 52 |
| (D) Orion Automatic | 364 | 52 | 392 | 56 |

(Larger cars available on request in both Ireland & Britain)

## RAILROAD PASSES IN IRELAND

Complete freedom of choice traveling as much and whenever you please for 8 or 15 days. Whether your destination is the Giants Causeway in the North, Blarney Castle in the South, Dublin City in the East or Connemara in the West, there is a train or bus service to take you wherever you wish to go.

Children Under 16 years deduct 50%.
(1) The **Emerald Card** provides unlimited travel on Rail and Bus both in the Republic of Ireland and Northern Ireland (including Dublin City Bus Services, Airport and Ferryport services).
(2) A Rail or Bus only ticket provides unlimited travel on the Irish Rail or Irish Bus Network in the Republic of Ireland (excluding Dublin City Bus Services, Airport and Ferryport services).
(3) The 8 day ticket allows travel on 8 days only but may be used over a period of 15 days. Similarly the 15 day ticket may be used for 15 days of travel over a period of 30 days. This means the days of travel need not be consecutive.

| | 8 Days | 15 Days |
|---|---|---|
| Emerald Card | $185 | $315 |
| Rail or Bus Only | 107 | 157 |
| Rail & Bus Combined | 139 | 203 |

# GENERAL CONDITIONS

**AIR TRANSPORTATION:** Non-refundable APEX tickets must be fully paid and issued not later than 30 days prior to departure—this is an airline regulation BUT we must receive full payment for air and land arrangements **45 days prior to departure.** The availability of seats at the non-refundable APEX fare levels are limited—so be sure to book early.

If a cancellation occurs within 30 days of departure or once ticket is issued, by airline regulation no refund will apply except in the event of death of passenger or member of passenger's immediate family appropriately substantiated. This regulation will be strictly enforced by the airline. No alteration may be made to tickets once issued.But please see our Tour Protection Plan on Back Cover.

Standard APEX fares are available on request—must be fully paid and issued no later than 21 days prior to departure. **Cancellation Fee: $75.**

**RESPONSIBILITY:** CIE Tours International. Inc. ("CIE Tours") 108 Ridgedale Ave., Morristown, NJ 07960 is not responsible for any personal injury. property damage or other loss you may suffer or incur on this tour arising from the acts or failure to act on the part of any Air Carrier. Public Transport Company. Hotel. Car Rental Company. sub-contractor or other person or organization, whether or not such air carrier, public transport company, hotel, car rental company, sub-contractor or other person or organization is rendering any of the services or accommodations offered or supplied on the tour. All tickets, coupons and orders are furnished and issued subject in all respects to the foregoing and to any and all terms and conditions under which the transportation and other services and accommodation provided thereby are offered and supplied. CIE Tours accepts no responsibility for losses or expenses due to delay or changes in schedules, sickness, weather, strikes. war. quarantine or other causes. All such losses or expenses will be borne by the passengers. Baggage is "at owner's risk" throughout the tour unless insured. Small articles (coats, wraps, umbrellas. etc.) are entirely in the care of the passengers. The right is reserved to decline to accept or to return any person as a member of any tour or to cancel or alter the tour. Airline liability for passenger baggage is limited by their tariffs.

**LAW:** The customer's contract with CIE Tours is subject exclusively to Irish Law and Jurisdiction for Irish Tours or English Law and Jurisdiction for British Tours.

**ACCOMMODATION:** Land arrangements will be provided as described in each individual tour. The right is reserved to substitute hotels, and sightseeing features listed herein for accommodations in similar categories as seasonal conditions may require. Accommodation in Farmhouses and Town & Country Homes is clean. comfortable and welcoming and does not include private bath or shower.

**TOUR DIRECTOR:** The entire land portion of all motorcoach tours will be conducted by a professional driver/guide and/or tour director as specified for each tour.

**VISITS, ENTERTAINMENT AND OTHER FEATURES:** Occasionally establishments indicated for visits. entertainment and other features are closed or cannot be visited for reasons outside our control. In such circumstances we will endeavor to provide an alternative.

**BAGGAGE:** All handling of one piece of luggage (size should not exceed 29" x 20" x 10") per person on coach tours is included in the fare. **Only one piece of luggage per passenger is permitted.**

**MEALS:** Meals are provided as specified in each tour program. Dinner menus in Irish and British hotels are Table d'Hote.

**DEPOSITS AND FINAL PAYMENTS:** A deposit of $100 per person per tour is required within 10 days of making telephone reservations (please quote your booking locator number when forwarding payments). Final payment is due 6 weeks prior to departure. If a booking is made within 6 weeks of departure, full payment must be made immediately.

MCO's (Miscellaneous Charge Orders) are not accepted for deposits but are accepted for **full payment** on credit card sales only and must be validated on Airlines nominated by CIE Tours. A processing fee may be applied, but this will be advised at time of booking.

**LATE BOOKINGS:** Subject to availability and conditions, you may book a tour between 30—14 days prior to departure. Overnight delivery charges will be assessed when necessary to provide documents for late reservations.

**REVISION FEE:** A $35 handling fee per booking will be applied for any revision made after the original booking has been made and processed. Revisions are not acceptable within 14 days of travel. The above revision fees apply to land bookings. see "air conditions" for costs to revise air reservations (where air tickets are already issued).

**CANCELLATIONS:** Advise of cancellation **must** be made in writing by post, telex or fax. Refund applications can only be processed upon return of documents. The following cancellation penalties are applicable:
**AIR:** See above "Air Transportation".
**LAND:** The following per person cancellation fees apply: **CANCELLATION NOTICE: Car Tours & Based Holidays—** Min. 45 Days: $50, 44/15 Days: $100, Under 15 Days: $150. **Escorted Coach Tours—** Min. 45 Days: $100, 44/15 Days: $150, Under 15 Days: $275.

**IMPORTANT:** For $49 per person you can protect yourself against the above liability with cover offered by "Insure America" (see Page 24 for details). An information sheet with details of inclusions/exclusions will be mailed with your confirmation.

**REFUND FOR UNUSED TOUR ARRANGEMENTS:** Unused hotel accommodations or any other unused service or feature of any tour are not refundable nor exchangeable for other accommodations. services or features unless agreed upon prior to departure.

**DOCUMENTS:** Documents will be shipped by U.P.S. approximately 25 days prior to departure provided final payment has been received. In the event that this is not acceptable we require sufficient notice in order to avoid express shipping charges.

**NOT INCLUDED:** All items of a strictly personal nature (such as room service. beverages. food not on regular menus, telephone and valeting charges. etc.) are not included and must be paid for by the passenger.

**OPTIONAL TOURS:** All optional tours featured in this brochure must be booked with the tour director and the additional fee(s) paid to him. Prices available on request. The right is reserved to cancel any optional tour should insufficient reservations be received.

**TIPS:** Tips for items of a personal nature, and to the Tour Director and Driver, are not included in the tour fare and are left to your discretion.

**TAXES:** All taxes imposed by local authorities. except airport boarding taxes. are included. The U.S. International Transportation Tax ($6). U.S. Customs Charge ($5) and U.S. Immigration Tax ($5) are not included in air fares.

**CHILDREN:** Children under 12 years of age cannot be accommodated on extended motor coach tours and children 12 years of age and over are charged the full adult fare and must be accompanied by an adult.

**ROTATION OF SEATS:** On all motor coach tours seats will be rotated at the beginning of each sightseeing tour or half-day of travel. The occupants of the front seats must move to the rear and all others will move forward one row.

**NON-SMOKING:** Smoking is not allowed on coach tours. Frequent sightseeing and rest-stops will be made at which time there will be opportunity to smoke.

**MOTOR COACH:** Motor coach tours are normally operated by 44 to 53 seater motor coaches. In the event of passenger bookings dropping below the minimum number of passengers, a smaller coach or mini-bus may be used.

**CAR RENTAL INSURANCE:** (1) Car rental charges include unlimited mileage and third-party insurance. which provides passenger indemnity in respect of injuries resulting from an accident involving the rental car. The driver of the car is **NOT** covered by this insurance but he can take out a personal accident insurance. (cover up to a maximum IR£4.000 in Ireland: UK£10.000 in Britain). to cover injuries received while driving on payment of an additional charge of IR£2.20 per day in Ireland and UK£2.00 per day in Britain.
(2) Under the insurance included in the cost of the car rental. the hirer is responsible for all damage to the rental car and must leave a cash deposit, or an imprint of a major credit card. with the car rental company at the commencement of the rental period to cover any damage which occurs. At the time of printing the deposit applicable in Ireland is IR£600.00 and in Britain UK£1.500.00 (all groups). This deposit will be refunded if the car is returned undamaged at the end of the rental period.
(3) The hirer can avoid the necessity of paying the deposit described in paragraph (2) above. and can indemnity himself against damage to the rental car (excluding the first IR£30.00 in Ireland). by taking out a Collision Damage Waiver at a supplementary charge which is non-refundable. The supplementary charges payable are: Ireland IR£8 per day. Britain UK£6.90 per day groups A to C: UK£11.50 groups C auto F. Except mini-bus which is UK£8.05 per day.
(4) All hirers in Ireland between 21 and 25 years must purchase the Collision Damage Waiver. Hirers in Britain between 23 and 25 years must pay an additional 50% of the cost of the appropriate Collision Damage Waiver.
(5) The insurance cover may exclude driving in certain countries. If the hirer/driver intends to cross the renting country border. he should check in advance with the car rental reservations office about possible restrictions.
(6) The additional charge for car rental days in excess of the number of days covered by the voucher issued by CIE Tours. will be at the rental brochure rate.
(7) All insurances are payable direct to the Car Rental Company in the local currency. Credit cards are accepted.

**AGE LIMIT:** In Ireland hirers must be over 21 years and under 70 years of age and must have at least 2 years driving experience. In Britain hirers must be over 23 years and under 70 years of age and must have at least one years driving experience. In Britain drivers 23 to 25 years are restricted to certain car groups.

**DRIVING LICENCE:** Drivers must produce a current driving licence issued in their state or country of residence (or an International Driving Permit) without any endorsements.

**GASOLINE:** The purchase price of gasoline is the hirer's responsibility and is not included in the car rental price. The rental car will be supplied with full tank of gasoline which must be paid for directly to the car rental company's representative at the commencement of the rental.

**MILEAGE CHARGES:** All self-drive tours featured in this brochure include unlimited mileage.

**IRELAND RAMBLER TICKETS AND DUBLIN EXPLORER TICKETS:** These are issued subject to the conditions outlined in the by-laws and regulations of the board of Coras Iompair Eireann.

**PARTICIPATING CARRIERS:** All airlines. Effective dates of operation of tours: 1st January through 31st December 1991.

## IMPORTANT NOTICE
**PRICES: all prices in this program are shown in U.S. dollars and are based on currency rates and fares existing on November 1st, 1990. Fares are per person based on sharing twin room. The Tour Operator reserves the right to alter prices at any time prior to your departure and without prior notice if, in their opinion, circumstances so warrant. Any devaluation or revaluation of currencies may affect the printed prices.**

# TOUR PROTECTION PLAN

**CIE Tours** has specially designed a comprehensive travel insurance package to protect you and your travel investment before and during your trip. Because we strongly recommend you purchase this valuable coverage, we will automatically include the cost on your invoice. Your confirmation documents will include details of the benefits. Once you purchase the Tour Protection Plan, you will receive a Certificate of Insurance. Please reveiw carefully as some exclusions apply. If you decide not to purchase the coverage simply sign the insurance waiver card provided and deduct from your payment.

## SCHEDULE OF BENEFITS

**Tour Cost, Trip Cancellation and Interruption** · (Total land cost & total airline penalty charge). Pays covered loss due to unforseen circumstances or death, injury or illness of you, a family member, or traveling companion.

**$500 Baggage and Travel Documents** · Pays for covered items lost, stolen or broken on your trip. Includes borrowed or rented property.

**$1,000 Medical Expenses** · Pays covered accident, sickness and emergency dental with no daily limits or deductibles.

**$5,000 Emergency Assistance** · Pays for covered evacuation and transportation as directed by a doctor to the nearest adequate medical facility.

**$10,000 Accidental Death and Dismemberment** · Pays for covered accidental death or dismemberment 24 hours a day while you are on your trip.

**TRAVEL GUARD Assistance** · On-the-spot medical assistance, medical evacuation… all just a phone call away.

**PREMIUM $49.00**
**(cover both Land & non-refundable Air)**

# COMBINE BRITAIN AND IRELAND

★ **London and Escorted Tours of Ireland**
★ **Self Drive Vacations Britain & Ireland Combined**
★ **London & Dublin Combined**
★ **Add Days in Britain or Ireland—Total Flexibility**

Fly British Airways to Britain—Tour Britain or Sightsee in London—then fly Aer Lingus to Ireland, tour by escorted coach tour or by self drive car—then home by Aer Lingus with onward connections if necessary.

—OR do it all in reverse.

Ask your Travel Agent for our 1991 book of Combination Programs to Britain and Ireland.

---

**Information and Reservations through your Travel Agent only**

Your travel agents will give you all the assistance you need in selecting any one of the tours described in this brochure. They're full of information and have the services which will assure you of a well planned itinerary. When booking your CIE Tour, look for this sign. It is a symbol of the American Society of Travel Agents. and an assurance that you are dealing with a reliable. qualified. and knowledgeable company you can trust.

**FOR AGENTS USE ONLY:**
**CIE Tours International**
      Tel (201)-292-3438
      Tel (800)-CIE-TOUR (Outside NJ)
      Tel (800)-447-0279 (NJ Only)
      Fax (201)-292-0463

**Your Travel Agent**

AAA WORLD WIDE TRAVEL
SCHUYLKILL COUNTY AAA CLUB
POTTSVILLE, PENNA.

# THE HOUSES
# AND CASTLES OF
# IRELAND

# ABERCROMBIE & KENT
## 1991-1992

Aer Lingus ☘

# DUBLIN, IRELAND
## AUGUST, 1990

Ironically, although Ireland is a country famous for literary genius and an ever-apparent "gift of the gab", no writer has ever quite succeeded in capturing the charm of the country on paper. James Joyce came close. So did Molly Keane, Sean O'Faolain, William Butler Yeats and Flann O'Brien. But even their best efforts were doomed to failure, for Ireland is an elusive enchanter whose glamour often lies in what is left unsaid, undone, unsung, unpublicized and untranslatable. In other words, you have to be there.

When you travel with Abercrombie & Kent, you will find that your itinerary is planned to give you ample opportunity to sample the charms of Ireland. In the cities you can visit great buildings and monuments of the 18th, 19th and 20th Centuries, take tea in a flowered parlor, amble through stately parks and squares, and shop for the country's famous crystal, lace and woolens. Out in the countryside (where you stay in some of Ireland's most charming and impressive country house and castle hotels), pass through centuries of history marked by moat and menhir, enjoy emerald landscapes bathed in misty light, join the singsong in a local pub and just simply relax.

The key to enjoying Ireland is to take it at its own pace—sipped, not gulped, as the locals say. We recommend that you make your trip as leisurely an excursion as possible, and that you come prepared to be captivated by a country whose friendly welcome, unique accommodations and delicious food will put you immediately at ease.

*Cead mile failte!* We hope to have the pleasure of your company in Ireland this year.

Jorie and
Geoffrey Kent

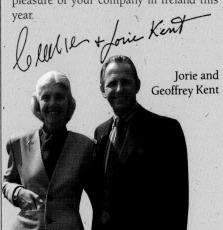

# THE HOUSES
# AND CASTLES OF
# IRELAND
## 1991

## Escorted Tour—Country Pursuits

### Magical Ireland
### 11 Days

**Land Arrangements** • IT1EIAK
Double Occupancy-price per person     $4590.00
Single Supplement     $ 950.00

**Airfare** Apex from New York     $ 603.00

# The Independent Traveller

### The Aristocratic Route
### 15 Days

**Land Arrangements** • IT1EIAK
**SELF-DRIVE** Automatic transmission vehicle with
superior accommodations     from $3960.00

**DRIVER-GUIDE** Private car and driver with superior
accommodations     from $7250.00

### The Irish House Party
### 9 Days

**Land Arrangements** • IT1EIAK
**SELF-DRIVE** Automatic transmission vehicle with
superior accommodations     from $2660.00

**DRIVER-GUIDE** private car and driver with superior
accommodations     from $4530.00

### The Houses and Hills of Ireland
### 14 Days

**Land Arrangements** • IT1EIAK
**SELF-DRIVE** Automatic transmission vehicle with
superior accommodations     from $3890.00

**DRIVER-GUIDE** private car and driver with superior
accommodations     from $7315.00

**Arrangements**
Quoted tour prices include planning, handling and operational
charges, and are quoted on the current rate of exchange and tariff as
of August, 1990. In the event of a marked increase in foreign
exchange or tariff rates, costs are subject to revision.

**Air Transportation**
Airfare quoted is that in effect August, 1990, and is subject to
change without notice. Advance purchase restrictions and cancellation penalties apply. Airfare is subject to high.season surcharge.

# TABLE OF CONTENTS

# AER LINGUS:
# FLY IRELAND TO IRELAND

Aer Lingus, the airline of Ireland, has more flights leaving for Ireland from the U.S. more often than any other airline. Service year round to both Shannon and Dublin, all on widebody aircraft, is operated from New York, Boston and Chicago and, starting in spring 1991, direct non-stop service will be offered from Los Angeles. Frequent and convenient Aer Lingus flights are provided to six other airports in Ireland as well as ten cities in Britain and twelve in continental Europe.

When you fly Aer Lingus you'll be treated to the kind of old-fashioned Irish hospitality that brings a smile to even the weariest face. Your Irish vacation begins the moment you set foot on the plane as you experience the special warmth and attention of Ireland itself from the friendliest cabin attendants in the skies.

So, fly Ireland to Ireland, and let Aer Lingus put the magic back in travel for you as we transport you to the magic of the Emerald Isle.

## ABERCROMBIE & KENT IN IRELAND

With our own A&K office "on site" in Dublin, Abercrombie & Kent is uniquely equipped to provide the best-designed itineraries and finest service available in Ireland. Our staff members are thoroughly familiar with the accommodations and attractions we recommend, and are always available to assure that your trip is smooth, trouble-free and effortlessly enjoyable.

## GUARANTEED DEPARTURES

This year we are again pleased to offer guaranteed departures on our escorted **Magical Ireland** program. Once we have received your deposit and your date has been confirmed, you have our guarantee that your program will depart as scheduled.

## TRAVEL WITH AN ESCORT

A&K offers two different but equally enjoyable approaches to travel in Ireland: escorted and independent itineraries. For those who prefer the convenience and companionship of an escorted program, we offer **Magical Ireland**, and 11-day exploration of the south and west. With just 12 passengers per departure, a "travelling house party" atmosphere prevails as you tour the countryside in a luxury coach, accompanied by an enthusiastic and knowledgeable guide.

## INDEPENDENT TRAVEL

Group travel—no matter how exclusive and companionable—is just not the thing for some independently-minded travellers. If you prefer to travel on your own, with family or with a small group of friends, A&K can easily plan a rewarding and carefree itinerary just for you.

Independent travel offers great flexibility and a wide range of transportation options. You can drive yourself: in a limousine, a luxury car or a more inexpensive manual or automatic shift model. Alternatively, you can hire a chauffeur or travel with a professional driver-guide. Whichever mode of independent travel you may choose, we help you prepare with information about the history, geography and attractions of the areas you visit. Our independent travellers receive detailed maps and a day-by-day sightseeing itinerary personally tailored to their own special interests and schedule.

## CUSTOM DESIGNED TOURS FOR GROUPS

Perhaps you have a special interest—in gardening, 18th Century architecture, Irish music or fox hunting—which you would like to indulge while on holiday. Abercrombie & Kent can plan a unique special interest itinerary for you, for your family, or for any club, museum or association group: an excellent chance to meet like-minded Irish people and to broaden the boundaries of your avocation. See your travel agent or A&K for details.

# DINING IN IRELAND

Ireland is famous for fresh vegetables and fruit, rich dairy products and fine seafood—most notably Dublin Bay prawns, salmon and trout. In recent years this abundance of fine ingredients has inspired a new group of talented young chefs influenced by the Continent but mindful of traditional, local favorites as well. In city and country, their menus offer great variety and excellent quality.

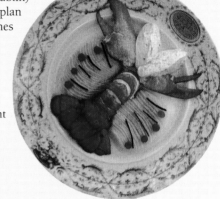

On our escorted program, **Magical Ireland,** breakfasts and dinners (except in Dublin) from a restricted a la carte menu are included in the cost of the program: a flexible plan which allows travellers to choose from interesting and varied dishes. Some lunches are also included, though many locations feature such tempting tearooms, country pubs and outdoor cafés that we have purposely excluded lunch from the scheduled program, to give you time and opportunity to explore for yourself.

On independent programs, lunch and dinner are not included, leaving you free to make your own selection of local restaurants. However, as we have found that our travellers appreciate the convenience, we do reserve a table for you on the night of your arrival at each country house hotel.

## COUNTRY PURSUITS: ESCORTED PROGRAMS IN BRITAIN AND FRANCE

In addition to our activities in Ireland, Abercrombie & Kent also offers a full range of escorted programs in England, Wales, Scotland and France. As on **Magical Ireland,** these **Country Pursuits** tours travel in small groups with a fully qualified guide (English-speaking in France), stopping at Britain's most charming country house hotels and in France's unique château hotels.

Explore Britain's southwest on **Legends of Sarum,** or see Wales and the Cotswolds on **Myths and Mountains.** Further afield, **A Scottish Sampler** provides an introduction to the scenic Highlands, while **The Grand Tour** takes you on a great circle route from London to Edinburgh. Across the water, **Le Coeur de la France** centers around Paris and the Ile de France while **Le Grande Tour de France** is just that.

For details, request your copy of the 1991 Abercrombie & Kent **Châteaux and Country Houses of Britain, Ireland and France** brochure.

# MAGICAL IRELAND

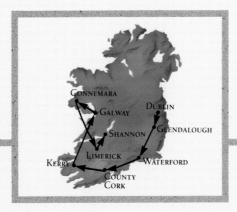

After an appetite-whetting tour around Ireland's capital city, you travel through County Wicklow for a first taste of the Irish countryside, known throughout the world for its "thousand shades of green." Gracious Glengarriff is your next stop, where the charming local accent welcomes you to Blarney Castle and a hospitable city.

The southern Ring of Kerry is a scenic paradise no visitor should miss, and you will spend a day exploring in this land of blue skies, shimmering lakes and rolling, misty hills. Turning northward along the coast, after an amble through cozy Connemara more unforgettable vistas unfold. The spectacular Cliffs of Moher figure in many an old Irish ballad, and near Galway The Burren is a unique alpine region famous for its wildflowers.

Along the way you experience Irish hospitality firsthand with accommodations in charming country house hotels, lunches at the private homes of local families, and cocktails at Thomond House, a classic example of Anglo-Irish elegance. Your last nights are spent in stately Dromoland Castle near Limerick, where you'll toast new friends and unforgettable memories at a special farewell dinner.

**DAY 1 FRIDAY** Individual arrivals in Dublin. Optional theater tickets can be arranged for this evening. *Shelbourne Hotel*

**DAY 2 SATURDAY** A morning tour of the city, with an afternoon excursion to Malahide Castle. *Shelbourne Hotel*

**DAY 3 SUNDAY** Powerscourt Gardens, the Glendalough Monastic Site, Russborough House, Cashel. *Cashel Palace Hotel*

**DAY 4 MONDAY** Waterford city, crystal factory or showrooms, Rock of Cashel. *Cashel Palace Hotel*

**DAY 5 TUESDAY** Blarney Castle, Glengarriff, Kenmare. *Park Hotel*

**DAY 6 WEDNESDAY** Ring of Kerry. *Park Hotel*

**DAY 7 THURSDAY** Adare Village, Galway city. *Ashford Castle/ Cashel House*

**DAY 8 FRIDAY** Connemara County. *Ashford Castle/Cashel House*

**DAY 9 SATURDAY** Cliffs of Moher, The Burren, County Clare, cocktail party at Thomond House. *Dromoland Castle*

**DAY 10 SUNDAY** Glin Castle, Limerick, farewell dinner. *Dromoland Castle*

**DAY 11 MONDAY** Departure on **Aer Lingus** from Shannon.

---

<u>SEE INSERT FOR FULL PRICE DETAILS.</u>

TOUR DATES (ARRIVE DUBLIN)

| 1991 | | 1992 | |
|---|---|---|---|
| ARRIVE | DEPART | ARRIVE | DEPART |
| Apr 26 | May 06 | Apr 24 | May 04 |
| May 17 | May 27 | May 22 | Jun 01 |
| Jun 07 | Jun 17 | Jun 26 | Jul 06 |
| Jul 12 | Jul 22 | Jul 17 | Jul 27 |
| Aug 02 | Aug 12 | Aug 07 | Aug 17 |
| Sep 13 | Sep 23 | Sep 11 | Sep 21 |

<u>YOUR LAND ARRANGEMENTS INCLUDE:</u>

All hotel accommodations as shown in itinerary; full Irish breakfasts throughout; dinner from restricted a la carte menu except on Days 1 and 2; lunches on Days 4 and 10; cocktail party on Day 9.

All sightseeing as shown, including entrance fees

All ground transportation, porterage and local taxes

Services of a Registered Guide throughout your trip

<u>NOT INCLUDED</u>

Are personal expenses such as beverages; laundry; phone calls; telexes; cables; gratuities to driver and guide; any additional sightseeing or meals not included in the itinerary; any airfares.

# The Country Houses and Castles of Ireland

DATING FROM THE DAYS WHEN NO SELF-RESPECTING ARISTOCRAT WOULD HAVE DREAMED OF FORGOING HIS COUNTRY SEAT, MANY OF IRELAND'S COUNTRY HOUSES AND CASTLES HAVE GAINED A NEW LEASE ON LIFE AS SMALL, PRIVATE AND EXCLUSIVE HOTELS. FAR FROM THE NOISE AND BUSTLE OF THE TOWN, WRAPPED IN THEIR OWN LOVELY GARDENS AND GORGEOUS VIEWS, EACH OF OUR RECOMMENDED PROPERTIES HAS BEEN CHOSEN FOR ITS HOSPITALITY, SERVICE, COMFORT, CUISINE AND LOCATION.

## The Shelbourne • Dublin

*To the Irish the Shelbourne is a legendary hotel, inextricably woven into the social, cultural and artistic life of the capital.*

*Overlooking the lakes and trees of St Stephen's Green in the heart of Dublin, the Shelbourne is only a few minutes' walk from the cultural, financial and shopping districts of the city. The building first opened its doors as a hotel in 1824 and since then has been immortalized by Thackeray and mentioned in dozens of memoirs and novels, including Joyce's Ulysses.*

*Now a Trusthouse Forte hotel, the Shelbourne has been fully restored to its early glory and to an unchallenged position as one of Europe's finest hotels. All 164 bedrooms (including 22 suites) are magnificently furnished and contain all modern comforts. Amenities include 24-hour room service, a beauty salon, valet service, hairdressers and barber, gift shop and an enclosed parking lot.*

*The Aisling Restaurant serves modern Irish cuisine; its elegant decor and courteous service combine to create one of Dublin's finest dining experiences.*

*The Lord Mayor's Lounge (an institution in itself) serves traditional morning coffee and afternoon tea, while in the Horseshoe Bar you'll discover that "there are no strangers in Ireland, only friends you haven't met."*

## The Westbury Hotel • Dublin

*Centrally located adjacent to Dublin's most fashionable shopping district, the Westbury is a five-star hotel of international standard, a member of the prestigious Leading Hotels of the World group.*

*This Doyle hotel has 200 bedrooms, each complete with private bath, hairdryers, direct-dial telephones, color television and complimentary in-house movies. There are also six luxury suites with whirlpool bath.*

*Just off the elegant lobby, visitors will find the Terrace Bar, the perfect place in which to relax before or after dinner. Alternatively, the Sandbank Seafood Bar offers both liquid and solid refreshment, in the form of an excellent variety of seafood dishes available at any time of day. The Russell Room features gourmet menus created by the hotel's Swiss-trained chef de cuisine.*

*Although the hotel is centrally located, visitors need not be concerned about parking: a complimentary underground lot is available to Westbury guests. In addition, the hotel also contains a convenient ground-level shopping arcade with an excellent range of Irish and European merchandise.*

## Park Hotel Kenmare • County Kerry

*The Park Hotel Kenmare is situated on the famed Ring of Kerry, set in eleven acres of beautiful parklands. Built in 1897, the hotel still retains its original Victorian character, with wood fires and fine antiques in the reception hall and drawing room.*

*This is one of Ireland's foremost luxury hotels. Spacious deluxe rooms are all individually decorated with period antiques. A Michelin-starred restaurant offers an excellent menu featuring fresh local produce, complimented by the room's superb view over Kenmare Bay.*

*The Park Hotel Kenmare was nominated by the Egon Ronay Guide for 1988 as the Best Hotel in Britain and Ireland. It is an ideal property from which to explore the natural beauties of one of the most scenic regions of Ireland.*

## Cashel Palace Hotel • County Tipperary

*In 1730, Bishop Bolton built a Palladian mansion near the town of Cashel, and for the next two hundred and thirty years his elegant home served as a bishop's palace. Today it has been transformed into a luxury hotel with elegant rooms and gourmet dining.*

*Recently refurbished throughout, all bedrooms in the hotel include a private bathroom and telephone, and the Cashel Palace's gardens are truly magnificent: with a "Queen Anne" mulberry planted in 1702 and hop bushes descended from an ancestor planted in the 1740's by Richard Guines (whose son was later to found the Guiness stout breweries).*

*The Bishop's Buttery is a popular meeting and eating spot, the Four Seasons' Restaurant is one of Ireland's finest, and for Irish hospitality at its best, visit the Cellar Bar.*

*The Cashel Palace's stated policy is "to send each guest away with a firm resolve to return." Elegant accommodations, friendly and attentive service, a convenient location and those spectacular gardens all combine to ensure that this is so.*

9

## ASHFORD CASTLE • COUNTY MAYO

One of the most luxurious residences in Europe, Ashford Castle rises majestically from the northern shores of Lough Corrib in County Mayo. Built in the 19th Century over a period of thirty years, Ashford was the country seat of Lord Ardilaun and the Guiness family until 1939, when it was converted into a luxury hotel. All eighty-three guest rooms and suites have been recently refurbished to the highest standards, each with a modern bathroom en suite.

Ashford is of particular interest to visitors who enjoy sports: there is an exclusive 9-hole golf course designed by Eddie Hackett; salmon and trout fishing; target shooting; duck and pheasant hunting; tennis; and horseback riding.

The hotel boasts two of the finest restaurants in the West of Ireland: the Main Dining Room offers superb continental and traditional menus, while the new Connaught Room specializes in French cuisine. In the Dungeon Bar, sip a pint or an Irish coffee while enjoying the music of piano or harp.

Near Galway, Connemara and the Aran Islands, Ashford Castle is an excellent base from which to tour some of Ireland's most beautiful and interesting countryside.

## DROMOLAND CASTLE • COUNTY CLARE

Just eight miles from Shannon Airport, Dromoland is one of Ireland's most famous baronial castles. Home for many years to the O'Brien clan, Barons of Inchiquin, the castle, now a luxurious hotel, still contains many reminders of their ownership, including portraits, statuary and a romantic walled garden.

Most of Dromoland's guest bedrooms, including suites and staterooms, have two double beds or king-sized beds with newly modernized bathrooms and full amenities. All are furnished with damask wallpapers, antiques and custom-designed carpets and drapes.

Dinner menus are in the classic continental manner, regularly featuring local prawns, sea trout, tender spring lamb and salmon. The wine cellar is stocked with an impressive list of fine vintages.

Dromoland Castle is famous for sport, which includes golf on the hotel's own 18-hole course, fishing, boating, tennis, and hunting, with horseback riding and deep sea fishing nearby.

With Bunratty Folk Park, King John's Castle and Craggaunowen Castle all within ten miles of Dromoland, the castle is an ideal vantage point from which to explore the Limerick/Shannon region. Killarney, Dingle and the Cliffs of Moher are also within easy reach.

## KILDARE HOTEL AND COUNTRY CLUB • COUNTY KILDARE

*The new Kildare Hotel and Country Club is designed to appeal to the most discerning guests. Only thirty minutes from Dublin, the property features elegant lounges, luxurious bedrooms and suites, a superb restaurant, swimming pool and health club.*

*Relax in its glorious setting of 330 private acres, strolling landscaped gardens and wooded corners, or challenge yourself on the Arnold Palmer-designed, 177-acre, 18-hole golf course due to be completed in July of 1991. Fishing and other sports are also available.*

## ELEGANT IRELAND

*For those travellers who wish to explore an area of Ireland in depth, **Elegant Ireland** offers a chance to rent a private home for a week or more.*

*Choose your pleasure: available properties are located almost everywhere in Ireland and range from a bijou flat in busy Dublin to a cozy cottage on the misty, mountainous coast. You can even spend some time as "lord of the manor" in a stately castle set in its own rolling parklands. Staff service is included in some rentals, and can be arranged if requested in almost all locations. Some properties have special sports opportunities including boating, bicycling, tennis or golf.*

*Whatever your taste, **Elegant Ireland** has the perfect "home" for you. This option is a particular favorite for family parties and group of friends travelling together.*

13

# I

THE
INDEPENDENT
TRAVELLER

FOR THOSE WHO PREFER THE FREEDOM AND
FLEXIBILITY OF INDEPENDENT TRAVEL, ABER-
CROMBIE & KENT OFFERS A WIDE VARIETY OF
CUSTOM-DESIGNED OPTIONS—INCLUDING SELF-
DRIVE HOLIDAYS AND TRAVEL WITH AN ACCOM-
PANYING DRIVER-GUIDE. THESE TAILOR-MADE
ITINERARIES ARE CUSTOM DESIGNED TO PRO-
VIDE JUST THE RIGHT PLAN FOR EACH
INDIVIDUAL TRAVELLER. WHEREVER
YOUR SPECIAL INTERESTS LIE, WE CAN
PLAN A HOLIDAY WHICH WILL FOCUS ON
YOUR PARTICULAR PURSUITS. OF COURSE, IF
YOU SIMPLY WANT TO REST AND RELAX, WE KNOW THE BEST PLACES FOR THAT EVER-
POPULAR PASTIME AS WELL.

• DRUMLEASE HOUSE

KILDARE HOTEL
AND COUNTRY CLUB
•
• ASHFORD CASTLE          • SHELBOURNE HOTEL/
• CASHEL HOUSE             WESTBURY HOTEL

                          • ROUNDWOOD

• DROMOLAND CASTLE/        • MARLFIELD HOUSE
  THOMOND HOUSE
                          • WEXFORD
• GLIN          • CASHEL PALACE
  CASTLE          HOTEL
              • LONGUEVILLE HOUSE

• PARK HOTEL KENMARE

# SELF-DRIVE HOLIDAYS

Hire the car of your choice and follow the detailed maps we provide to the country house hotels on your itinerary. With our detailed documentation and Ireland's excellent road system, a self-drive holiday is easy and carefree.

In conjunction with Johnson & Perrott and Avis, A&K offers a wide selection of rental cars. Cars listed in each category are examples only and similar models may be substituted. A valid U.S. or Canadian driver's license is required for driving in Ireland.

A. Ford Fiesta (stick shift)
B. Opel Corsa 2-door (stick shift)
C. Opel Kadett 4-door (stick shift)
D. Opel Vectra (stick shift)
E. Estate 5-door (stick shift)
F. Toyota Corolla (automatic transmission)
G. Toyota Carina (automatic transmission)
H1. Ford Granada (automatic transmission)
H2. Mercedes 230E (automatic transmission)
J. Eight-seat Minibus (stick shift)
L. Nissan Micra (automatic transmission)

The price of your self-drive program includes unlimited mileage and, with the exception of some cars, VAT (Value Added Tax). CDW/PAI insurance and petrol are not included and are payable directly.

# DRIVER-GUIDED HOLIDAYS

Travel with your own personal escort, who will drive a provided vehicle and use his or her own expertise to add to the enjoyment of your trip. These professionals are licensed guides who will show you parish churches, stately homes and antique shops you might otherwise have missed. Another bonus: you need never worry about finding a parking spot! A variety of vehicle categories are available for driver-guided programs. Prices include the services of the guide, his/her expenses, government taxes and petrol.

**Small Parties And Special Interest Group Programs**
Luxury coaches and minivans are available for small parties of friends travelling together, or for clubs and special interest groups. These include a Volkswagen Minibus with 8 seats plus driver and small luxury coaches with 15 seats plus driver.

**Program Documentation**
Before departing for Ireland, independent travellers receive complete, personalized information for their program. On arrival in Ireland, additional information, including detailed maps, is ready and waiting for you.

**Prices quoted for self-drive and driver-guide programs include:** all accommodations in country house hotels as detailed in your personal itinerary (based on rooms in the hotels of your first choice or similar), Value Added Tax and service at most hotels, self-drive car or driver-guided touring arrangements as explained above. A full Irish breakfast daily is also included.

**Not included:** transfers between your Dublin or Shannon hotel and the airport (unless specifically requested); lunches and dinners; gratuities to hotel porters; cost of obtaining passports or other required passenger documentation; and personal expenses such as beverages, laundry or phone calls.

To help you begin planning your holiday, we offer the following suggested itineraries in Ireland.

# THE ARISTOCRATIC ROUTE

Arrive in Dublin, for centuries the social and cultural hub of Ireland, to stay at one of the city's most elegant (and centrally-located) hotels. The Irish have a long tradition of "going up to town" for a shopping expedition, a trip to the theater or a special celebratory dinner: you have time to explore shops, museums and galleries—or the beaches a mere thirty minutes away.

South and east lies County Wicklow, where the magnificent gardens of Powerscourt and Fernhill await. Visit the ancient monastic site at Glendalough, the crystal factory at Waterford and one of the oldest towns in Ireland, Wexford, before the road takes you to Cashel. Here, at the end of a leisurely drive, visit The Rock and its ecclesiastical ruins, Cahir Castle and—if you wish—nearby Cork and Fota Arboretum.

Heading south, touch your lips to the famous Stone at Blarney Castle near Kenmare, said to confer the gift of eloquence to all who kiss it. Further south Bantry Bay offers beautiful views and the Garnish Island Gardens, a local favorite. Then you'll explore the Ring of Kerry, 120 miles of spectacular coastal and mountain scenery.

After a relaxed drive through lovely County Clare—and perhaps a stay at palatial Dromoland Castle—scenic Connemara beckons with its lakes, mountains and bogs. Visit historic Kylemore Abbey or Westport House, a fine 18th Century mansion. Explore Sligo, Lough Gill, Rosses Point and Yeats country, including the poet's burial place at Drumcliff. En route back to Dublin, stop at Carrigglas Manor in Longford, to see a fine collection of costumes in the house's Victorian style.

Ireland's aristocrats were once famous for their ready hospitality and charming manners, for their quiet country retreats and serene gardens. **The Aristocratic Route** shows you that these qualities are very far from extinct in the modern republic.

**DAY 1** Arrive in Dublin from London or USA. *Shelbourne Hotel/ Westbury Hotel*

**DAY 2** Exploring in Dublin and environs. *Shelbourne Hotel/ Westbury Hotel*

**DAY 3** County Wicklow: Fernhill Gardens, Powerscourt and Glendalough. Overnight in Gorey. *Marlfield House/Private home in the Wicklow Hills*

**DAY 4** Sightseeing and shopping in Waterford and Wexford. *Marlfield House/Private home in the Wicklow Hills*

**DAY 5** The craft workshops of County Kilkenny and Cashel's The Rock. *Cashel Palace Hotel/Longueville House*

**DAY 6** Cahir Castle, Fota Arboretum and Cork City. *Cashel Palace Hotel/Longueville House*

**DAY 7** The Blarney Stone; Bantry House and Garnish Island Gardens on Bantry Bay. *Park Hotel Kenmare*

**DAY 8** The Ring of Kerry. *Park Hotel Kenmare*

**DAY 9** Relaxing in County Clare. *Dromoland Castle/Private home*

**DAY 10** North to Connemara. *Cashel House Hotel/Ashford Castle*

**DAY 11** Connemara's Westport House or Kylemore Abbey. *Cashel House Hotel/Ashford Castle*

**DAY 12** Drive to County Leitrim's Sligo, Lough Gill and Yeats country. *Drumlease Glebe House*

**DAY 13** Sightseeing among Yeats landmarks: Sligo town, Rosses Point and Drumcliff. *Drumlease Glebe House*

**DAY 14** Return to Dublin, stopping at Carrigglas Manor en route. *Shelbourne Hotel/Westbury Hotel*

**DAY 15** Depart on Aer Lingus for the United States or London.

---

*· See Insert For Self-Drive and*
*Driver-Guide Prices*

Per-person prices are based on two persons travelling together and vary according to car type and accommodations chosen.

See page 14 for a complete listing of self-drive car categories.

We recommend that you contact your travel agent or A&K for the most recent Aer Lingus airfares.

# THE IRISH HOUSE PARTY

Travel on an **Irish House Party** itinerary is a unique experience. These independent programs combine the country house hotel network with stays in private family homes. What better way to get to know a country than through its people, their homes and lifestyles? Here you stay for a night or more in period or historic houses, as the exclusive guest of friendly, interesting hosts.

The sample itinerary which follows begins in Dublin and works its way south and west to Limerick. Though none of the better-known sights—such as Powerscourt, Waterford and Bunratty Castle—are slighted, there is also a particular emphasis on charming smaller towns and gardens. At each stop, you benefit from congenial company, attractive surroundings and the best of Irish cuisine: common characteristics of all **Irish House Party** homes.

Please remember the private houses featured here do not have all of the facilities found in large hotels: if you would sorely miss 24-hour room service or a heated swimming pool, perhaps another option would be best. However, if you are curious about and interested in life as it is lived in other countries, and if you would like an opportunity to meet Irish people (and their horses and dogs!) on a one-to-one basis, you will thoroughly enjoy **The Irish House Party.**

Because these are private houses, we cannot guarantee that a particular residence will be available at all times. However, we can almost always find an interesting host in the area of your choice, for your holiday dates.

**DAY 1** Arrive in Dublin and transfer to an idyllically located country cottage just 25 miles from the city, in the Wicklow Hills. *Roundwood*

**DAY 2** Local sightseeing at Powerscourt, the Glendalough monastic site and Russborough. *Roundwood*

**DAY 3** South to Enniscorthy on the Slaney River, then to New Ross and on to spend the night at a charming country house in Wexford. *Wexford*

**DAY 4** The crystal factory at Waterford, then a drive east to Dungarven, Cork and on to coastal Kinsale. Here you may stay at the home of a Cordon Bleu cook or in a delightful guest house overlooking the harbor. *Kinsale*

**DAY 5** Exploring in Kinsale, or drive to Timoleague to visit the local abbey and nearby gardens. *Kinsale*

**DAY 6** Drive through Killarney to County Limerick, with a stop at Muckcross Gardens en route. Stay at a magnificent castle, home to the Knight of Glin. *Glin Castle*

**DAY 7** Head back to Dublin via Limerick and Bunratty Castle, and through counties Tipperary and Kildare. Stay in the heart of Dublin or at a country club west of the city in Straffon. *Westbury Hotel/Shelbourne Hotel/Kildare Hotel and Country Club*

**DAY 8** Sightseeing in Dublin: theaters, museums, art galleries and shops abound. *Westbury Hotel/Shelbourne Hotel/Kildare Hotel and Country Club*

**DAY 9** Depart on **Aer Lingus** for the United States or London.

THE
INDEPENDENT
TRAVELLER

14 DAYS

CONNEMARA
DUBLIN
COUNTY CLARE
KERRY WEXFORD
COUNTY CORK

# THE HOUSES AND HILLS OF IRELAND

Once arrived in Dublin, you begin your tour in this lovely city on the Liffey. The 18th Century turned Dublin into an elegant European capital, while the 19th gave it splendid museums, libraries and art galleries. Nearby is the influential Georgian Country House of Castletown, and Malahide Castle, once seat of the ancient family of Talbot, now housing part of the National Portrait Gallery.

Then drive southeast, to explore the contrasting faces of Ireland—the majestic garden terraces of Powerscourt and the monastic ruins of Glendalough, where seven churches cluster around two lakes in honor of St. Kevin. The next day is devoted to old Ireland, as you visit Kilkenny, the Rock of Cashel, mountain seat of the King-Bishops of Munster; and Cahir, castle of the Butlers, Dukes of Ormonde.

Heading west, a pleasant drive takes you through the heart and soul of rural Ireland. You stop at Cork and perhaps Riversdown House with its exquisite stucco, before arriving in Kenmare. Here, amidst a landscape as lovely and lonely as could be wished are Bantry House, with the art collection of the second Earl; the Italianate island garden of Garinish; and Killarney, with its stunning landscapes.

Now travel north—through Limerick; Killaloe at the foot of Lough Derg; and Galway, where Columbus prayed in the Cathedral on his way to the New World—to your base amid the loughs and mountains of Connemara. Here you can fish, boat or play golf. Finally, it is south once more to the beautiful ruins of Kilconnel Friary; across County Clare is Dromoland Castle, a Gothic wonder where you relax for a day before departing from Shannon Airport.

The symbol of Ireland is the shamrock, but if you find a four-leafed clover you'll be lucky enough to return some day.

DAY 1 Arrive in Dublin from London or USA. *Westbury Hotel/Berkeley Court Hotel*
DAY 2 Georgian Dublin. *Westbury Hotel/Berkeley Court Hotel*
DAY 3 The Wicklow Hills. *Marlfield House*
DAY 4 The Wicklow Hills and Wexford. *Marlfield House*
DAY 5 To the heart of Ireland. *Cashel Palace Hotel*
DAY 6 Rural landscapes. *Longueville House*
DAY 7 County Cork. *Longueville House*
DAY 8 To the far southwest. *The Park Hotel*
DAY 9 The Ring of Kerry. *The Park Hotel*
DAY 10 North to Connemara. *Cashel House/Ashford Castle*
DAY 11 Loughs and mountains. *Cashel House/Ashford Castle*
DAY 12 From Connemara to County Clare. *Dromoland Castle/Thomond House*
DAY 13 Exploring and relaxing. *Dromoland Castle/Thomond House*
DAY 14 Depart on **Aer Lingus** for the United States or London.

*See Insert For Self-Drive And*
*Driver-Guide Prices.*
Per-person prices are based on two persons travelling together and vary according to car type and accommodations chosen.

See page 14 for a complete listing of self-drive car categories.

We recommend that you contact your travel agent or A&K for the most recent Aer Lingus airfares.

# Terms and Conditions

All quotations are outlined in the price insert, and include the following:

### 1. Accommodations
Deluxe and first-class hotel accommodations as per the special selection of hotels made by Abercrombie & Kent. If one of the specified hotels is not available, an alternative hotel of similar standard will be booked.

### 2. Meals
Breakfast, dinner (except in Dublin) and some lunches on escorted tour; see individual itinerary. Meals are not included on independent travel arrangements, except for full Irish breakfast.

### 3. Baggage
Handling of one piece of baggage per person is included on escorted program. On self-drive and driver-guided programs, gratuity for porterage is at your discretion.

### 4. Transportation
Self-drive cars are provided by Avis or Johnson & Perrott. Terms and conditions for each are detailed on page 14. For escorted tour, transportation will be in the most modern and practical vehicles available.

### 5. Taxes and Gratuities
Hotel taxes and service charges are included when possible. (A few hotels do not include service, preferring to leave gratuities to the discretion of the guest.) VAT on most self-drive cars is included: see page 14 for details.

### 6. Entrance Fees
Entrance fees to parks, museums and homes are included on escorted program but not on self-drive and driver-guided programs.

### Not included in quoted tour prices:
Cost of obtaining passports or other required passenger documentation; personal expenses such as beverages, laundry or phone calls.

### Registration
For escorted program: A deposit of $500 per person is required at the time you book. The remainder of the cost of your trip is due 60 days prior to your departure date. If your reservation is made within 60 days of departure, the entire cost of the trip must be paid at the time of confirmation.

For independent travel: A non-refundable deposit of $250 per person is required at the time reservations are requested. The remainder of the cost of your trip is due 60 days prior to your departure date. If your reservation is made within 60 days of departure, the entire balance must be paid at the time of confirmation.

When your reservation is initiated within 30 days of your departure, a non-refundable "rush booking" fee of $50 per booking will be charged.

### Cancellations
For escorted program: Cancellations received 60 days or more prior to departure will be subject to a $100 per-person cancellation fee per tour or extension. Cancellations received less than 60 days prior to departure will be subject to the following forfeit of cost per tour or extension: 59-45 days, 10% of tour cost; 44-14 days, 20% of tour cost; within 14 days, 100% of tour cost.

For independent travel: Cancellations received 60 days or more prior to departure will be subject to a $250 per-person cancellation fee per tour or extension. Cancellations received less than 60 days prior to departure will be subject to the following forfeit of cost per tour or extension: 60-30 days, 30% of tour cost; within 30 days, 100% of tour cost.

Trip cancellation insurance is strongly recommended; see details on this page.

### Refunds for Missing Days
All claims for days missed on vacation should be made in writing within 30 days of termination of the trip. This claim should be accompanied by a certificate of service from the Tour Operating Company stating that the days were indeed missed. Refunds are based on the actual costs of services involved and not on a per diem basis. Refunds will not be made for unused sightseeing trips or meals.

### Responsibility
ABERCROMBIE & KENT INTERNATIONAL, INC. is an Illinois corporation which books travel arrangements with various independent overseas ground operators. Each of these companies is an independent corporation with its own management and is not subject to the control of ABERCROMBIE & KENT INTERNATIONAL, INC. For convenience, these and other independent ground operators are sometimes referred to in this brochure as "correspondent companies."

All bookings are accepted by ABERCROMBIE & KENT INTERNATIONAL, INC., as agent for independent overseas ground operators like those described above. The transportation, accommodations and other services provided by the ground operators are offered subject to the terms and conditions contained in the tickets, exchange orders or vouchers issued by them and/or their suppliers. Because ABERCROMBIE & KENT INTERNATIONAL, INC., does not have the right to control the operations of the independent operators and their suppliers, IT CANNOT BE LIABLE FOR ANY PERSONAL INJURY OR PROPERTY DAMAGE which may arise out of these services.

ABERCROMBIE & KENT INTERNATIONAL, INC. reserves the right to cancel any itinerary or any part of it, to make such alterations in the itinerary as it deems necessary or desirable, to refuse to accept or to retain as a member of any tour any person at any time, and to pass on to tour members any expenditure occasioned by delays or events beyond its control. In case of any appreciable variation in its costs, ABERCROMBIE & KENT reserves the right to adjust its rates.

### Air Transportation
Airlines concerned are not to be held responsible for any act, omission or event during the time passengers are not on board their planes or conveyances. These tours may use the services of any IATA carrier. The passage contract in use by these companies when issued shall constitute the sole contract between the companies and the purchaser of these tours and/or passage.

International airfares and schedules are determined by the airlines. Concerns about costings or schedules should be addressed to the airline or to the agent who made the arrangements. Abercrombie & Kent International, Inc., cannot be held responsible for problems arising with airfares or air schedules.

All scheduled airline flights are occasionally subject to overbooking or cancellation. If this occurs, A&K and/or its correspondent companies will do all in their power to assist clients in boarding flights or finding alternative arrangements. It must be stressed that this is done as a courtesy to clients and A&K cannot be held responsible for denied boarding, nor for the additional costs thus incurred.

---

### Insurance In Ireland
Abercrombie & Kent's insurance administrator has designed a policy exclusively for A&K clients: a comprehensive travel insurance program underwritten by National Union Fire Insurance Company which offers coverage for trip cancellation or interruption, illness, injury and damage, loss or theft of baggage, as well as 24-hour worldwide emergency assistance, all specifically formulated with A&K programs in mind.
We strongly recommend that you insure yourself and your property while travelling. The cost of this program, and all coverage terms, conditions and exclusions are fully detailed in the description of coverage which will be sent upon confirmation of your tour reservation. If you wish further information, please contact BerkelyCare, our insurance administrator, at 1-800-343-3553.

ABERCROMBIE & KENT INTERNATIONAL, INC.
1520 KENSINGTON ROAD
OAK BROOK, ILLINOIS 60521
1-800-323-7308
(IN ILLINOIS 1-708-954-2944)

# THE WORLD
## with Abercrombie & Kent

For the past 29 years, the name "Abercrombie & Kent" has meant "simply the best way to travel" throughout Africa from Victoria Falls to the Pyramids.

Today, it is a name that means so very much more.

Today, you can travel almost anywhere in A&K style: Africa, Antarctica, the U.S.S.R., Australia and the South Pacific, Indonesia, the Orient and China, Europe, Egypt, India, the Galapagos Islands and Turkey—by air, private luxury train, canal barge, luxury cruise boat or hot air balloon.

So this year, whether you're planning a visit to Leningrad...Lake Naivasha... Laos...or Kyle of Lochalsh... call your travel agent and ask about Abercrombie & Kent. Wherever you go, we remain "simply the best way to travel" in comfort and style.

Any or all of the Abercrombie & Kent brochures shown are yours, with our compliments. Simply use the card bound into this brochure for your request.

**For more information contact:**